This year marks Sch
it is to celebrate our cen
the power of reading. A l
heart of everything Scho   ...ow us
what an essential, affirm.... ....y....s contribution reading makes in
our lives.

Reading is a way for us to reach out to you, and a way for you to reach
both within yourself and out to the wider world. Reading connects to
everything you experience, everything you dream about, everything you
know, and everything you might not know. When you read, you open up
your heart and mind to words and ideas...and your heart and mind
become so much stronger because of that.

Every day, words spread from Scholastic to reach millions of you in
classrooms, at home, and in libraries throughout the world, so that you
can have the moments of understanding, empathy, and community that
stories and information can bring into your life.

I want to thank all the authors here for their contributions, as represen-
tatives of the hundreds of thousands of voices that Scholastic has been
honored to share with the world over the past hundred years. I also want
to thank all the people who've worked at Scholastic during this time,
dedicated to making the world a better place through the power of
reading.

Mostly I want to thank you, the reader—because the ultimate power of
reading lives within you. You share this incredible milestone and a shining
moment with our company. Here's to all the reasons to love reading...and
to the power of reading to continue to grow for us all.

—Dick Robinson
Chairman, Scholastic

...Scholastic's 100th anniversary, and how wonderful ...Bicentennial with a hundred of our authors honoring ...love of reading and a belief in the power lie at the ...Scholastic does, and together these authors show us ...reading, and joyous creativity...

100 REASONS TO LOVE READING

by 100 Scholastic Authors

edited by David Levithan

Scholastic Inc.

ISBN 978-1-338-68170-3

10 9 8 7 6 5 4 3 2 1   20 21 22 23 24

Printed in the U.S.A.   40
First printing May 2020

Book design by Baily Crawford

Table of Contents

Editor's Note

by David Levithan

I love reading because reading is many acts of connection all at once.

It is made from the connection an author feels to the characters and the story.

It is made from the connection the author feels to the reader, and the author's hope that the reader will take something—meaning, enjoyment, self-worth, imagination—from the words that have been put on the page.

It is made from the connection the reader feels to the characters and the story, and the way the reader can take thoughts that have sprung from a stranger's mind and feel how they apply to the reader's own life.

If you read the right words at the right time, they can make you feel more at home in the world and more at home in yourself.

The authors in this book were asked to share a single reason they love reading. As you'll see, many of them went back to when they were kids, and certain stories made all the difference to the course of their lives. Others talk about seeing what the books they've written have meant once the connection was made with a reader. In these pages, you will see how reading can save lives, change lives, make lives better, and bring people together, whether they are in the same family or have never met before. A word that comes up a lot is magic, and I understand why, because the connections that reading can make are the closest thing to magic that I know.

As you'll probably figure out pretty quickly, the reasons here are arranged alphabetically by the authors' last names. The numbering is not meant to be a ranking—#94 is just as important as #2. Hopefully this is a book you can dip into from time to time . . . or read in one big gulp, if that's how you choose. (That's another great thing about reading—you get to decide how you want to do it.) And if you like what an author has to say, or the way that they've said it, I encourage you to check out their books, some of which are listed at the end.

The simplest connection you can have to a book is to pick it up and open it. If you're reading this, that connection has already been made. Thank you for being here.

Now, read on!

Reading has always been my greatest refuge, uniting me with people who've lived different lives and who can offer solace and wisdom.

Nothing makes me prouder than to think Hogwarts has been a similar refuge to others.

—J.K. Rowling
February 2020

"And just look at these books!" said Hermione excitedly, running a finger along the spines of the large leather-bound tomes. "*A Compendium of Common Curses and Their Counter-Actions*... *The Dark Arts Outsmarted*...*Self-Defensive Spellwork*...wow..." She looked around at Harry, her face glowing, and he saw that the presence of hundreds of books had finally convinced Hermione that what they were doing was right. "Harry, this is wonderful, there's everything we need here!"

And without further ado she slid *Jinxes for the Jinxed* from its shelf, sank onto the nearest cushion, and began to read.

from *Harry Potter and the Order of the Phoenix*

1. Reading gives you the power to understand

by K.A. Applegate

If you can read this sentence, congrats. You are in possession of the most amazing superpower on the planet.

Nothing as mundane as something you'd find in the MCU or the DC Universe. None of that invisibility or telekinesis stuff. No turning into animals after you acquire their DNA.

Nope. This is way better.

Reading gives you the power to *understand.*

To understand others. Your family. Your friends. Your dog.

To understand yourself. Your moods. Your fears. Your hopes.

To understand the world. The present. The past. And most importantly, the future.

Maybe you're thinking, *Meh. I'd rather be able to morph into, say, a red-tailed hawk.* (And yeah, that would be pretty cool.)

But here's the thing. When you understand the world, you can change the world. And in case you haven't noticed, the world could really use some changing.

Superpowers evolve in strange ways. Maybe you're bitten by a radio-active spider. Maybe you travel to Earth from another planet. Maybe you touch a glowing blue cube.

Or maybe you simply open a book and begin to read.

How does your reading superpower work? Well, as you read, you become part of the story. You imagine. You empathize. You participate.

Participation. That's what separates reading a book from all other forms of entertainment. Movies and TV show you. Books *need* you.

Movies and TV show you the action, the setting, the characters. There it all is, right in front of you on the screen. Filmmakers lay it out for you, like a meal in a restaurant, all cooked and plated and garnished.

Books don't do that. The difference between a book and a screenplay is that the screenplay is a set of instructions for a whole bunch of other people: producers, directors, casting agents, cameramen, stunt coordinators, wardrobe folks, props guys, tech wizards . . . on and on it goes.

When you read a book, all of those jobs are yours. You aren't just a bit player. The whole enterprise depends on you and your imagination.

Movies and TV are incredible. But let's face it, your pet cat can watch TV. It's not that it isn't involving, but you can sort of turn your brain down to a low setting and watch a TV show. You aren't contributing; you're just watching. Your name does not appear in the credits.

Ah, but with a book, you're necessary. You fill in the gaps, expand the ideas, make characters live. A screenplay cannot come alive without a whole crew of professionals.

A book needs just you.

Every time you read—every time you participate in a story—you understand the world just a little bit better. The more you read, the more your superpower grows, and the more you can change yourself and the world around you.

Now get to work. The universe needs you.

No pressure.

2. Reading shows you how to be gone

by Avi

When I was a boy growing up in Brooklyn, New York, living with my family, attending the local public school, I lived (as far as I knew) an ordinary life. There weren't many escapades in my life. No adventures. I don't recall ever being punished, at home or in school, for doing anything wrong. I wasn't timid. I just didn't do the things I had been told not to do. In short, my world was not very eventful or exciting. It just was. My biggest problems: I was much shorter than my twin sister, and I couldn't spell.

I did spend good times with my friends, listened to the radio (a lot), played stoop ball, and read books. Lots of them. It was the books that levitated me into another world.

I'm not sure when I first read Kenneth Grahame's *The Wind in the Willows*. That I loved the book is attested to by the fact that I still own my childhood copy. The friendship of Mole, Ratty, Badger, and Otter was, I thought, akin to my own friendships with Richie, Philip, and Mike, my best friends. But it was Mr. Toad who was my hero. What an unlikely hero! Spoiled rich, bombastic, a thief, a liar, self-centered Mr. Toad. Nothing like me, and yet, and yet, how *wonderful* he was. How delightfully charming, how thrilling, how exciting to be him, oh wonderful Mr. Toad. How fantastic that, in spite of all those bad characteristics (perhaps I haven't listed them all), I could be all those things—in my head.

Then there was *Treasure Island*. I was amazed by how Jim Hawkins—surely just my age, out on a high seas adventure in search of buried treasure—defeated the gang of murderous pirates, saved the good adults, found the treasure, discovered the castaway (mad Ben Gunn), and became friends with Long John Silver, the wicked—oh, was he wicked!—pirate chief. The thrill of being Jim in the apple barrel when he learns of the evil plots of the pirates! The murderous struggle with Israel Hands, high in the ropes and masts of the good ship *Hispaniola*! His bravery. His resourcefulness. His easy way with adults. If I couldn't be Mr. Toad, maybe I could be like Jim.

Ever since I read these books, I have tried to write such great books. I never will.

But I'll read *The Wind in the Willows* and *Treasure Island* again and you won't be able to find me. Don't even look. I'll be gone.

3. Reading opens your mind

by David Baldacci

I was born and grew up in Richmond, Virginia, a place that was largely segregated along racial lines at the time. The *Brown v. Board of Education* decision, in which the Supreme Court ruled that separate but equal was inherently unequal and that schools must be integrated with all due speed, came down in 1954. Virginia was the first southern state to abide by this urgent edict. I was part of the first class to be integrated. It was 1972. The "speed of a glacier" analogy would have done a disservice . . . to glaciers.

Simply because the separation of the races was no longer legal didn't mean that people's views changed. For much of my youth, many of the folks I knew would find any notion of true equality absurd. And any thought of this ever changing, despite the ruling from the Supreme Court, was considered even more outrageous. It was the way it was because it was always the way it was, a civil war and a civil rights movement notwithstanding.

As a college student, I would pass down Monument Avenue, Richmond's most prestigious broadway, and see each day the enormous statues of Confederate generals and political leaders erected there, glorifying those who fought to maintain slavery. Later came a long battle and angry protests when there was a movement to add another statue to Monument Avenue, that of native-born Richmonder and world-renowned African American activist Arthur Ashe. At that point we were very near the start of the twenty-first century, with incredibly heinous prejudices lingering still.

Those tenacious and insidious beliefs could have been mine as well. But my way out of this closed loop of thinking and living was reading books, specifically at the public library where my parents took me, my brother, and my sister every weekend. I checked out far more tomes than

I was supposed to, because the librarian knew I would devour all of them and be back the next week for more. I read about people who didn't look like me, eat like me, dress like me, learn like me, pray like me, or sound like me, but were nonetheless exactly like me in all important respects, namely in their humanity.

It has been my experience that readers are more tolerant, more curious about life, more open to changing their opinions on things, and, most importantly, more empathetic to others regardless of where they came from. Mark Twain once said that travel is fatal to prejudice, bigotry, and narrow-mindedness. He spoke from experience because he was the most traveled person of his time. But for those who lack the opportunity to circumvent the world on a whim, "travels" can be done by simply opening a book. Plane travel has made the world smaller. Yet books have always made the world available for all to experience, without the hassle of long TSA lines and crammed flights.

I might be a very different person today, if I were not a reader. I might be the sort of person that the current me would not like to be around. But I'm not, because I opened a book.

And so can we all.

4. Reading is a purple crayon

by Blue Balliett

Holding a book you can't forget—one that delights and haunts you—can equal holding power. This I know to be true!

As a kid, I was shy but deeply curious. Questions and big ideas chased each other around my mind. Sometimes I think the person I was when I first fell in love with books is exactly who I still am: an escapist Wonderer with a What-If view of things. Reading stories reassured me that the world was a big place, with many ways of seeing and doing—and plenty of Unrecognized Thinkers like me.

I believe with all my heart that reading the right book at the right time—at any age—can lead to finding a path in the real world. For me, this goes back to Crockett Johnson's *Harold and the Purple Crayon*, which I first experienced at four years old. Thick crayon in hand, Harold creates an exciting world that he then explores. When his purple lines begin to take over, he draws himself back out and returns home to his own bed.

What Harold did is what every writer does, but I didn't realize this for years.

As a kid, someone most definitely without power, I climbed into book after book. When E.L. Konigsburg's *From the Mixed-Up Files of Mrs. Basil E. Frankweiler* came out, I was twelve years old. Growing up in New York City and knowing that the Metropolitan Museum of Art was a real place, I couldn't get over the thrill of this story. For years after reading that novel, I imagined myself as a cooler, braver Blue within my familiar world, a person tackling puzzles involving great art. Someone who could get things done! Filled with hope and an ambition to fix what seemed wrong, I felt certain that books proved this could happen.

Decades later, I began writing stories that I wanted in my home as a parent and in my classroom, as a teacher—books about kids who tackle possibilities that the adults around them have missed. These kids visualize what needs to happen and then chart their way through some tough problems. I realize that all of my books grew from mysteries rooted in the real world. *Chasing Vermeer, The Wright 3, The Calder Game, The Danger Box, Hold Fast, Pieces and Players, Out of the Wild Night . . .* My awkward, determined characters all seem to be partly me, armed with serendipity and a handful of challenges that belong to us all. In my writing, I return again and again to questions about the meaning of art, of home, of dreams and unexpected friendship—and about the ways people navigate a change that tips their lives upside down.

I can't imagine who I would be without all the reading I've done—or what a world without books would be like. I believe that lives are built from the earliest stories we've loved. Does this mean that my world as I know it began with a single purple crayon?

5.
READING IS HALF THE FUN   BY JIM BENTON

6. Reading makes you an interesting person on an interesting journey

by Judy Blundell

A few years ago, my family underwent an upheaval. We moved from a small village to a new town. My daughter was twelve at the time, and I went through some considerable mom agony at the thought of her starting a new school in the middle of the school year. There is no doubt in my mind that I was in my worst mom-cheerleader mode—*What a great school! Let's look at clubs you could join!*—but I was just as nervous as my daughter, because *I remember middle school.*

So picture this: It is a gray January day. From the car, we watch the other kids surging into school, a jostling, teasing, laughing crowd, and she is nervous and I am worse, and I ask with sudden terror, "Will you have to eat alone in the cafeteria?"

And she says: "Don't worry about me, Mom. I'll be fine. I have a book."

I watched her go that day, shouldering that hundred-pound backpack as well as her shyness, her fear, and her courage . . . and the clouds parted, and the angels sang, and I thought: *She'll be okay. She has a book.*

Because with a book we are never alone.

I know what you're thinking: *What about our digital devices?* Go ahead, look at a screen when you're alone. You're not fooling anybody. You're just someone trying to look busy.

Ah, but if you hold a book? An actual book, with a cover that someone can peek at? You are silently and powerfully announcing that you are an interesting person in the middle of an interesting journey.

Books are portals. Books are escape. Books are comfort. Books are all of these things, but they are also a way of demonstrating your absolute cool. I know what you're thinking: *You're a writer, so of course you think this.* But I'm telling you, while everyone else is looking at a phone to watch a cat video (and I love a good cat video, don't get me wrong, but stay with me here), with a book you are lost in an invented world. You are with animals who talk and people who fly. You are with thieves and dragons and invisible dogs. Or you are learning deep truths about your own world. You are learning about who you are.

And what is cooler than *that*?

Let's time travel to another day. I am nineteen. I have arrived at college a few days early. The campus is empty, but the library is open and air-conditioned. I wander to fiction, starting with *A*. This one book at eye level practically falls into my hand. It is Jane Austen's *Pride and Prejudice*, a book I'd read in eighth grade and had not enjoyed. As a matter of fact, I resented that baffling book for even existing.

I open to the first page and begin to read. I laugh. I sink down on the floor and finish the chapter. I finish the book the next day. I take out another Austen. Then another. By the time classes begin, I have decided to change my major from journalism to English. Because I cannot imagine anything better than this.

That decision changed my life. It made me a novelist.

Reading the right book at the right time can keep you company or change your life.

Try it. Especially on a day you feel weird or squishy or left out. You'll be fine. You have a book.

7. Reading works whenever you get to it

by Coe Booth

I was a writer before I was a reader.

Yeah, I was *that* kid at school, the one who was always kind of in her own world. I mean, I was having so much fun creating characters and writing about *their* lives, who had time for mine? Even in second and third grade, I was happier writing than, well, doing anything else!

When I think about it now, it's hard to figure out why I didn't read. It should have been a natural fit. If you like to write, you should like to read, right?

Um, no. Not really.

At that time, books seemed out of reach for me. They didn't exactly *pull* me in their direction. Honestly, I thought books just weren't for kids like me.

Rarely did I see books about people who looked like me. And when they looked like me, they didn't live where I lived or do the things I did. The characters and the stories seemed so far away.

So I wrote the kind of stories I wanted to read.

I wrote about black girls in the city, girls who were sometimes going through hard times at home or with their friends. I wrote about girls who got their hair braided, who played double Dutch, and whose parents sometimes struggled to make ends meet.

More than anything, I wrote about girls who, like me, were just trying to figure themselves out.

I was doing all that writing, but I still wasn't reading.

Luckily for me, in fourth grade I found Judy Blume. Her novel *Are You There, God? It's Me, Margaret.* was the first book I really read on my own, just for me. The main character looked nothing like me, and she definitely wasn't from the Bronx, but a lot of her story was my story. She was a girl around my age who was growing up and wanted her life to make sense. Just like I did.

This was the first book I savored. *Loved.* It was the book that broke through. I guess you could say it was the key that unlocked the whole new world of books for me. I didn't know it at the time, but it was the key I had been waiting for.

After that, I read everything! I think I was trying to make up for lost time. There were so many books I wanted to read. *Needed* to read.

And it wasn't too late!

Now, many, *many* years later, I'm still writing the stories I like to read, and I sometimes get letters from kids who are also coming to reading a little later than most people.

I received an email from a boy who wrote, "I'm fifteen years old and your book is the first book I ever read, like, for real. I read the whole thing."

Talk about full circle!

Imagine that little girl in the Bronx growing up to write something that's a key for someone else, a book that hopefully will unlock a whole new reading world for another kid. I can't even tell you how exciting that is.

The good thing is, it really is never too late to become a reader.

8. Reading brings sage advice

by Ann E. Burg

The house was a grand old dwelling with a large, rolling lawn and great armchair stoop with a sycamore tree out front. Three families lived in it—our apartment was in the middle—two large bedrooms, a living room, dining room, kitchen, bathroom, and sunroom. The sunroom with its yellow walls and brown wicker chairs was my favorite, but it was the dining room that had the small window overlooking my world—my stoop, front sidewalk, and much-loved sycamore.

Brooklyn was the center of my universe. Everyone I loved lived inside its leafy borders and I knew every crack in the pavement, every neighbor who passed by on their way to and from work or school. On Sundays we'd visit Grandma, and every two weeks, my mother, brother, and I boarded the big green bus that would bring us to the library.

Why do you always bring home the same book? my brother asked whenever I found *Little Pear* stuck in the stacks again. Why wouldn't I? Though he lived far away in a one-room house made of sunbaked bricks, in a village surrounded by bean and cabbage fields, Little Pear was my friend. I couldn't just leave him squeezed on a library shelf, barely breathing, unread and unloved.

When we moved to New Jersey, there were lots of trees—a whole woods right in our backyard. But no favorite sycamore. No sunroom. No stoop. No big green city bus. I could sit on the curb for hours with only squirrels, birds, and bugs to keep me company.

And Max, the king of all wild things, was lonely and wanted to be where someone loved him best of all. Finally! Words to label the floaty feeling I sometimes felt with my New Jersey friends.

Books help me understand the world. They build bridges to people and places we might not otherwise know. "You never really understand a person," Atticus tells Scout in *To Kill a Mockingbird*, "until you consider things from his point of view." Every time we open a book, every time we care about a character, we build empathy with others and gain a deeper understanding of ourselves.

Even now, when my voice feels small and inconsequential, I remember the pale-looking angel with three freckles on his right cheek and a policeman's badge on his green corduroy shirt. I was five years old when I met him in *Ben and the Green Corduroy Angel*, the shiny blue book with the crackled spine. "What you do and say means something," the angel says. "Not just to me but to everyone you know." Good advice for all of us. Loud or soft, shy or not so shy, our voices are important.

Sometimes the world is leafy and lovely and we are surrounded by everything—sidewalk cracks or cabbage fields—that makes us feel safe and loved. Other times the world is strange and scary.

"Life is a struggle and a good spy gets in there and fights," Harriet explains in the book *Harriet the Spy*.

More sage advice from the pages of a book. For me this is the perennial joy of reading!

9. Reading can introduce you to the people you need in your life

by Kacen Callendar

To be honest, I was an extremely lonely kid. For years I wasn't accepted at the private school I attended as the Black and local student; other locals didn't accept me because I spoke like a "Yankee," or like a person from the States. I always felt like an outsider, and I really didn't have any friends.

Well, I didn't have any friends who were *real*, anyway.

I didn't know it then, but books were my friends. The characters from countless stories who went on endless adventures were the people who kept me going. When I was a child, the fact that I was so ostracized that my only friends were imaginary was devastatingly embarrassing—but I'm grateful for that now. Reading teaches empathy, and I met an array of people I might not have ever met otherwise. From the time I'd reached middle school, I was the only person in my class who would yell at anyone who ever said anything homophobic, not yet knowing that I would grow to identify as both queer and trans myself. This definitely didn't help the bullying or ostracization, but I was able to learn how to love others—and, even if I hadn't realized it yet, I was also learning how to love myself.

My mother would read to me almost every night when I was young. Some favorites as a five-year-old were the Berenstain Bears and the *Good Dog, Carl* board book. As I got older, my mom would read the Animorphs series to me. This is the first time I remember being so excited about a book that I would jump up and down on the bed, screaming in excitement, arms flailing. Besides the extremely intense plot (alien slugs in brains!) and amazing cast of characters, I was really excited because Animorphs introduced me to Cassie, a Black girl who was smart and kind and loved by her friends. It was the first time I saw an author decide that someone who looked like me was important enough to be the hero who saved the world. To this day, Cassie remains one of my oldest and closest friends. Whenever I think of her, I feel a wave of courage and strength, the same feeling I'd have if someone were to remind me that I'm worthy of being loved and respected, and that I belong.

Cassie isn't real, but the love her author put into her character is real. Cassie might not be a person outside the pages of the books I still have in my childhood home's closet, but that love transferred from her creator and was put into words. That love spreads through every young reader who reads the books. My imaginary friendship with a series and a character became a tool of self-love. It's the same tool I wield every time I sit down to write a book. I hope to transfer that same love in my words, and to create characters who will be friends to any reader, young or old, who needs them most.

10. Reading is the magic found

by Sharon Cameron

The year of my eleventh birthday, I lost a treasure. Fifteen dollars.

In 1981, fifteen dollars was vast wealth. Untold riches. An amount that could transform my summer, because it was the last installment needed to buy my longed-for ten-speed bike. My pink birthday card with a white-and-purple swan printed on its front had been full of dreams. Now it was empty. The money had vanished, and I was left with the certainty of impending doom. My mother was going to be mad. Very mad.

So I didn't tell her. I made a million excuses about not buying the bike, shut the door to my room, and read books all summer instead.

I have book crushes. I first realized this during my bike-less summer. I fall in love with a book and read it over and over again. In the days when checking out a library book meant signing your name on the little card that slid into the paper pocket inside the back cover, it secretly pleased me to see my own signature there, stacked up line after line. The book might belong to the library, the plot and characters to the author, but the story was mine. All mine. In some magical way, a story that had been part of someone else had become part of me.

There's a wonder and a mystery in this. That summer, for the first time, I understood a little of the magic, and I gained so much more than I had lost.

Last year, I picked up one of those books I fell in love with when I was eleven. It was about an ancient house with ghosts in its cellar, and a secret tunnel that crossed the lane to a graveyard, where an old woman sat on her knees and lovingly washed the tombstones. And the book talked about time. How time was like an old wall, built stone upon stone, with hard, irregular, unchanging pieces that somehow managed to sit side by side and create something beautiful.

It was so me.

It's no wonder my eleven-year-old soul was thrilled by that book. I'm still thrilled by it. These are the ideas I write about now. Ancient places, secrets, extraordinary people, things that time should never be allowed to forget. Because long ago, during a long, empty summer, magic traveled from an author to a book to a reader. I was changed, and now that same magic travels back out into books again. This is the never-ending circle. A magic that was, is, and will always be, as long as there are readers and authors, and as long as there are books.

And so it's no wonder I went back to the library that summer I was eleven, my fingers trailing along the spines, and pulled that book once again from the shelf. It's not so strange that I put my signature beneath the stack of my signatures already on the card. It's really no mystery at all that I took that book back home to my room, opened it, and saw my fifteen dollars tucked between the pages.

I had gained so much more than I found. And that is magic.

11. Reading is good trouble

by Angela Cervantes

When I was a kid, I used to get in trouble for reading too much. It's true. I'd lug books everywhere I went, including to the dinner table. In between bites of chicken enchiladas or forkfuls of spaghetti, I'd read. I'd read right up until my mom would call out my full name: "Angela Christina Cervantes! Put the book away now and eat dinner!" As my siblings giggled, I'd stash the book away before my mom could warn me a second time. A second warning was really a final warning. There would be no third warning.

Only once did I ignore that first warning. I was reading E.B. White's *Charlotte's Web* at the dinner table and thought I had time to read just a little bit more before my mom put her foot down. It probably didn't help that my mom had served pork for dinner and I wasn't planning on touching it—in honor of Wilbur, of course!

With the second warning, the book was snatched out of my hands. I didn't get the book back for a full two days. Pure torture!

At school visits, I tell kids about how I used to get into trouble for reading too much. Most of the students and teachers nod in recognition when I admit this fact.

"How many of you have ever gotten into trouble for reading too much?" I ask.

Hundreds of hands fly up, eagerly wanting to tell me about the time a favorite book got them into trouble. Once, a student said he was busted reading *Captain Underpants* at church instead of listening to the sermon. Another time, a kid said she stayed up reading my book *Lety Out Loud* all night under her covers while the rest of her family slept. She woke up dead tired the next day.

"Was it worth it?" I asked.

"Yes!"

Then there was the kid who admitted to me and his entire fifth-grade class that he pretended to be sick one day just so he could miss school and finish *Holes* by Louis Sachar. His teacher just smiled with a glimmer of pride in her eyes.

After listening to kids' stories about the level of sneakiness they'll go to, to keep reading, I proudly tell them, "You're my people." It's no joke. Readers are exactly the kind of troublemakers who will always be my people.

The truth is, reading made me a writer. And when I sit down to write, I write with the colossal hope that my book will be so good and so loved that a third grader isn't going to be able to put it down at the dinner table, even after they've been warned multiple times. I hope that a fourth grader is going to lug my book to their place of worship and get so busted for it. And somewhere out there, way past bedtime, a fifth grader is going to sneak my book under the covers and read, read, read until they've finished the last line. This idea fills my heart with joy. Is it awful that I strive to create book-loving troublemakers?

Don't answer that.

The fact is, reading is good trouble. It's the kind of trouble we should all be getting into. You can tell your parents I said that.

12. Reading conjures new landscapes

by Lucy Christopher

I found my love for reading in a hot, strange land when I was nine years old. I was curled up in the back of a Holden station wagon with Elyne Mitchell's *The Silver Brumby* clutched tight. I was reading about Thowra, a wild stallion who steals away domestic mare Golden, then shows her his magnificent bush home in the Snowy Mountains. I knew if I kept my head down reading, I wouldn't have to talk to everyone else.

The *everyone else* was the Bolwell family we'd just bought a house from, who were taking me camping. Strange, perhaps, to go away with our house's previous owners, but I'd been in Australia only a few months and didn't have any other friends. Claire was a year older than me and her sister, Sarah, a year younger—instant *besties*, perhaps. But they were everything I was not—they slathered Vegemite onto their crackers and wiggled it through the holes, they swam like fish in their own pool, and their dad took them camping. We didn't own a pool, or a tent, or Vegemite. I hadn't had a dad for a while either; part of the reason for moving was getting to know him.

On the drive, Mr. Bolwell joked about snakes, spiders, hot days and freezing nights—all that awaited us camping. I picked up one of Claire's books, discarded in the footwell, and hid in its leaves. Land and time are very long on Australian road trips; it's possible it took the same amount of hours to finish the book as to reach our destination. Mitchell's *The Silver Brumby* was a dream I sank into in sprawling Melbourne suburbs and awoke from in a mountainous national park. Perhaps I blinked when I did so, the forests and granite tors of Mitchell's book conjured to reality.

I devoured more of Mitchell's series on future camping trips. Soon I read them aloud to Claire and Sarah by flashlight to a background of cicadas. I loved that nature in Mitchell's books was not calm or typically

English—instead wind roared, horses ran wild, and landscape was unpredictable. Mitchell's awe-filled descriptions made me observe the land I was in with fresh interest, too. Soon, I saw my first snake, laughed with the others at wombat poo outside our tent, and even witnessed my own wild brumbies. My previously tightly wound roots were feeling a tentative path through Australian dirt; I was connecting with the land I'd been so scared of.

Mitchell's rich imagery continued to pull me through those early years, her words like crumbs leading me deeper into the bush. She showed me something magical and wonderful in Australia, and the Bolwell family helped me find it. During a school trip months later, I was first to volunteer for the bush walk challenge.

When I wrote my first novel, *Stolen*, I recalled my early reading of Mitchell's Brumby books. I remembered that in *The Silver Brumby*, Thowra shows Golden the beauty and power of his home; he wants her to love it and live with him inside it. *Stolen* is also about a young female kidnapped to wild Australian land and encouraged to love it, this time a human girl rather than a horse. Perhaps, then, my childhood reading of *The Silver Brumby* gave me more than I realized—not only encouraging my love for Australian land, and also its literature, but also sowing seeds for my own novel. Mitchell's *The Silver Brumby* made me need and depend on reading in a new and exciting way; Mitchell also made me love a land so much that I had to write about it myself.

14. Reading taps into knowledge

by Suzanne Collins

My family has a tradition we call Fall Weekend, which is misleading. It's really Fall Afternoon. When the leaves are peaking in Connecticut, we drive around to see the beautiful foliage, stop at an orchard to sip hot cider and eat doughnuts, and lay in a supply of apples.

This year, I impulsively bought a packet of maple candy, each piece prettily molded into the shape of a maple leaf. I'd always wanted to try it because of a book I'd loved as a child, *Understood Betsy* by Dorothy Canfield Fisher. In the book, nine-year-old Betsy, after a hard day at school, comes home to find her grown-up Cousin Ann boiling down maple sap into syrup. She's given a cup of the hot syrup to pour in loops and curves onto packed snow to make candy. They called it waxed sugar. *Concentrated sweetness of summer days was in that mouthful, part of it still hot and aromatic, part of it icy and wet with melting snow.* Yum.

My daughter remembered them making maple candy on plates of snow in Laura Ingalls Wilder's *Little House in the Big Woods* and pouring the syrup into pans to harden into sugar. Our maple leaves were more like the latter, crunchy and grainy and dissolving deliciously on our tongues.

Neither of us had ever tapped a maple tree for sap, boiled it into syrup, or made candy, but we knew about it from books we'd read as kids. I found out that you can dye white fabric with tea from the All-of-a-Kind Family series, and Encyclopedia Brown taught me that if you can spin an egg like a top, it's hard-boiled.

So many things I discovered reading books were like seeds that grew inside me and then blossomed in my own work. *Alice's Adventures in Wonderland* inspired Gregor's tumbling through a grate in his laundry room to a world beneath New York City in the Underland Chronicles. The siege of Leningrad in *Boris* introduced me to the concept of using starvation as a weapon, which takes many forms in *The Hunger Games*. And Betsy's family making maple syrup? That came back in *Catching Fire* when Katniss uses a spile to tap a tree for water when she's desperately thirsty in the arena.

When you are lost in a story, without even noticing it, you are soaking up knowledge like a sponge. I love reading books because you effortlessly learn things that can stay with you for a lifetime.

15. Reading is a shared journey

by Bruce Coville

When I was a kid, my father was a traveling salesman, which meant he was away from home fairly often. The natural result of this was that time with him was a valuable commodity, one that my sibs and I struggled over.

We didn't perceive Dad as a reader—at least, not of books. But one night, for reasons I have never understood (though it occurs to me now that it might have been due to a nudge from my mother) he took me into the living room, opened a thick brown book called *Tom Swift in the City of Gold*, and started to read to me.

In doing so, he opened not just a book, but the world.

Was it a great book? No, not really. Was it a great story? Oh yeah!

But the greatest thing about it was sharing that time with my dad. Night after night he took me along on this adventure with Tom and his friends as they traveled underground in search of the mysterious City of Gold. It became *our* adventure, too.

Flash forward twenty-some years and I'm a dad myself, reading a book for a college class on fantasy literature. My five-year-old son, who is feeling out of sorts because there is a new baby in the house, climbs up next to me and says, "What are you reading?"

"It's called *The Hobbit*."

"Read it to me."

"I don't think you're ready for it."

"Read it to me!" he demands, in a way that only a five-year-old can.

So I turn back to the beginning and start reading aloud, figuring he'll soon get tired of it.

Two weeks later we finish the book, having shared an adventure that carried us all the way to the Misty Mountains and into the cave of the fearsome dragon Smaug. And for weeks after that we play Hobbit, with my son being Bilbo and me being all thirteen dwarves.

Jump ahead again. I am about to drive cross-country with the baby mentioned above. She is now fourteen. Knowing that the two of us will be in the car for thousands of miles over a period of weeks, we stock up on audiobooks. Driving from coast to coast and back again, my daughter and I see an array of awesome and wonderful things. But for both of us, one of the strongest memories of that thirty-years-ago trip is the stories we listened to as we traveled, stories we experienced together that have become a shared memory.

We tend to think of reading as being a solitary activity. But whether it is a dad or mom reading to their child, a teacher reading to his or her class, two or more friends reading a book at the same time, or an older sibling reading to younger, reading *together* is one of the most powerful ways I know to forge a lasting connection with another person.

I love reading by myself, hunkered down in a chair and living in a story. I truly do. But for me, one of the most fabulous things about reading is that it is something you can do with friends and family, binding you in the spell of story and creating a connection or a shared memory that can last for the rest of your lives.

16. Reading enables you to learn from a world of authors

by Christopher Paul Curtis

There are two reasons I'm so much in love with reading, one personal and one professional.

Professionally, I love reading because every time I pick up a book, I rediscover the fountain of youth; I'm thrown back in time and become a student again. With each page I turn, decades fall away and I become ten-year-old Christopher sitting in Mr. Alums's English class awaiting that day's lesson.

Everything I read, from the finest literature to the slightest piece of fluff, becomes a lesson. I'm instructed on ways to make my writing more similar or less similar to what I'm reading.

I am so grateful to be living at this time because in spite of the many downsides of technology, it's easy to forget that it wasn't that long ago that books and the ability to read them were rare. Only the wealthiest individuals had the time, education, and finances necessary to take advantage of this marvelous skill. My ancestors were forbidden by law from learning to read. But we're living in an age where we have a relative embarrassment of riches, where libraries have become the great equal-izers, making books and authors available to all.

I can go to the library and get a book written by Toni Morrison or Walter Dean Myers and love the book for the way it reads. But I also get a free lesson from Ms. Morrison on how to move a scene around, and Mr. Myers can teach me how to make a reader feel a certain way. When or where else would I be able to do that? That's one of the reasons I love reading.

Personally, I love reading because I am a human being, and a large part of being human is finding a great deal of comfort in belonging to a group, a team, or some other form of family. For me, reading is the yellow-brick road that leads to that comfort.

When I read a book, I am given confirmation of a theme that runs through much of literature: In spite of superficial, cosmetic, trivial differences, you and I are much more similar to the other seven-and-a-half billion people on Earth than we are different.

One of the ways reading accomplishes this is because a well written book is nothing less than a magical tool that allows us to see inside another person's intimate thoughts, giving us a bit of insight as to why they feel the way they do.

Being an author is a very different job than most; even though a book is the result of many, many people working many, many hours, the creative process, where an author uses his or her words to say something, is usually done alone. Most authors work by themselves—it's hour after hour of you and your computer or you and your pen and paper.

By reading, I am able to invite any author I choose, contemporary or long gone, into my home to teach me how to become a better writer. And the best part is that I have a great time while I'm learning.

What's there *not* to love about reading?

17. Reading comforts and heals

by Edwidge Danticat

M te konn renmen lapli.

"I used to love the rain," a ten-year-old boy tells me when I ask him how the massive 7.0 earthquake that struck Haiti on January 12, 2010, killed three hundred thousand people, and left a million and a half homeless, had changed him.

Now the rain has become his enemy, he tells me, a kind of terror. Rain now means lightning that struck and killed a baby in his displacement camp. Rain now means that the floor on which he sleeps turns to mud. Rain now means sometimes standing up all night in fear of floods.

Another thing that has changed in the lives of the children who are read to on a weekly basis by the passionate Haitian readers of the Port-au-Prince–based Li, Li, Li! (Read, Read, Read!) reading-out-loud program?

Nou pa t konn cho kon sa.

"We weren't always so hot," some of the children say. "We did not always live in a tent."

In the midst of such sadness and turmoil, why read to displaced children who live in tents? I ask the readers, some of them homeless themselves.

"We read to these children for the same reason people read to other children," the readers say. "We read to them to help them grow their imagination, to teach them about the world around them. And beyond them. We also read to them to comfort them and to help them heal after this terrible disaster."

A few months after the earthquake, I had the honor of reading *Eight Days*, an English-language picture book I'd written about the earthquake, to the displaced children in a tent camp often visited by Li, Li, Li! readers in Port-au-Prince. The book tells the story of a little boy who survives the same earthquake that had devastated these children's lives. The boy survived after spending eight days in the rubble of his house, while using his memories and imagination to keep himself hopeful. I read *Eight Days*, using the pictures, while doing a simultaneous translation in Haitian Creole. Though I was afraid of upsetting the children by reminding them of the trauma of the earthquake, they were braver than me in addressing the issue at hand.

"Has someone close to you ever died?" one girl asked me.

"Yes," I answered.

"In the earthquake?" another asked.

"Yes."

"Who?" the boy who loved the rain asked.

I told him about my cousin and his son, who was about his age. Our family house had collapsed on top of them, I told him, and they had not survived. And for a moment this boy and I had a brief conversation that we might not have had were it not for the story.

"Has the earthquake changed you?" he asked me.

Not expecting that question, I stuttered.

"It's changed us all," I ventured before turning the question back to him. And that's when he told me about the rain, a common memory for both of us—mine decades old and his, only months old—of a head turned upward and a mouth opened toward a once-benign sky pouring out "good" rain. Much like the sky once did for another boy, my dead cousin's dead son, as well as the young survivor I had written about in my book.

Could a book ever teach a child to love the rain again?

Probably not.

Can books offer comfort and perhaps even help a child (and an adult) begin to heal after such a catastrophic event?

I sure hope so. Actually, now I know it's definitely possible.

18. Reading is good medicine

by Sayantani DasGupta

When I was in practice as a pediatrician—a doctor for babies and young people—I used to write prescriptions for reading. Every time a family of a baby or toddler came to see me for their checkup, I would take out a special prescription pad and write *read to your baby twenty minutes a day* on it and then present the family with a book that they could take home and enjoy together.

Why did I do this? Why did I prescribe reading, in the same way I might write down the name of a medicine to treat an ear infection or a stomachache? Because I knew, just like doctors all around the country who still do this know, that stories are good medicine. Reading together as a family helps teach words and language, helps bond families together, and helps children not only read earlier but learn to love books for a lifetime.

But, as I know from experience, reading can be good medicine in other ways too. Stories can be a place of imagination and escape. When I was growing up as a daughter of immigrants from India, there weren't a lot of other kids who looked like me or whose families had moved from countries far away, like mine had. I had a number of really good friends, but I had a lot of bullies too. These were kids who said mean things to me because my family spoke a different language or ate different food, or because my skin color was a dark brown. I found a lot of comfort by escaping into stories, and imagining myself in different time periods, or different universes, or inside different characters.

Unfortunately, even though I loved them, there weren't a lot of people who looked like me in the books I was reading or the movies and TV shows I was watching either. That lack of seeing myself in stories made the bullying more painful at some level. Even as reading was a way to escape, not seeing myself represented made me wonder if kids like me didn't deserve to be the heroes of books, or even the stars of our own stories. Which was a wrong and painful idea, of course, but I still thought it.

When I grew up and had kids of my own, I realized that I never wanted my kids or any other kids to feel this way. I wanted stories to be not just an escape, but a source of strength! So I decided to write my Kiranmala and the Kingdom Beyond stories for the twelve-year-old I used to be and for my own kids—so they could see a brown immigrant daughter being awesome, fighting monsters, cracking jokes, and saving the multiverse! I wanted to tell my kids, and all kids who read this series, that superheroes come in all genders, colors, and backgrounds. In fact, to solve the problems of the world, we're going to need all the different heroes we can get!

Reading helps us learn. It helps us escape. It helps us grow strong. It helps us imagine. Reading is good medicine in so many ways—for us, for our world, for the multiverse.

When we read, we can imagine not only new heroes but new ways for the world to be: more fair, more just, more full of love and laughter and acceptance. When stories fully represent our todays, they help us dream better tomorrows for us all.

19. Reading lets you know that you, too, have a story to tell

by Lulu Delacre

Why love reading? ¿Porqué amar la lectura? When you love to read, you hop from one book to another. From worlds of shapes, colors, and numbers to those of cars, planes, and trains. You dwell on drawings of beautiful birds, incredible insects, magnificent mammals, and fabulous fish. You cross roaring rivers and wander through woods. You climb marvelous mountains and gaze back at footprints tattooed in a golden sand dune. You go underwater without getting wet. You travel through space without missing a breath. You visit with dinosaurs that lived long ago and listen to creatures still to be born. You discover churches and mosques, royal palaces and humble huts. And as the art in the book gives way to thousands of words, you stumble on that special story, the story with which you connect. When you love reading, you leaf through so many pages that you end up realizing that you, too, have a story to tell.

I know for a fact that every reader is a writer at heart. I've read aloud stories set in Spanish-speaking countries or within a Latinx home life. I've gazed up from the page to look at the young audience in front of me. I've seen that sparkle of understanding in the kids looking back. In them I see you. I see when you click with a main character speaking words in español. You connect to a short story that celebrates family traditions like yours. And so it is that although you think you have nothing to say, out of fear of making mistakes, you know you also have lived like the story's hero did. You've cried and laughed. You've feared and conquered. You've failed and succeeded. You've imagined and dreamed. You are the main character of your own life. And so you can weave your past into fiction. It's only a matter of learning my trick.

At schools nationwide I give children some tools. I say, "Think of your favorite foods, for everyone eats. Think of a dish you can't wait to taste once again, on that annual holiday that calls for sharing it among family and friends." This is the request that prompts scores of hands to go up. "Hallacas, tamales, pupusas, burritos, pasteles, mangú, arroz con leche" are a few of the answers I've heard in the past twenty years. So I hand you the recipe I learned from Virginia Hamilton, a remarkable writer who came before me. It's the same one that I've given to hundreds of readers like you: Use what you remember, what you know, and what you imagine might happen next. Put words onto paper and tell your family story, for everyone has a story to tell. You see, one day your brand-new short story may turn future readers into writers as well.

20. Reading leads to a world of infinite adventures

by Chris D'Lacey

It may seem strange, but I barely read a thing when I was young. My parents had no interest in books. We were not a reading household. Occasionally, I would pick up a Marvel comic and lose myself in the superhero world. But books were never on my horizon.

All this changed one afternoon when I was fourteen. I was sitting in an English class, bored. My teacher, Mr. Sidney, was pacing the room, reading to us from Shakespeare. Mr. Sidney was an elderly scholar. He wore a brown flannel suit, dusted with chalk marks. While he droned through *Hamlet*, I had my hands in my lap, fingers interlaced, thumbs twirling like a small turbine. Mr. Sidney stopped by my chair. He said, "Can't you do *anything*, boy, but twiddle your thumbs like that?" I replied, "Yes, sir; I can twiddle my thumbs like this." And I turned the turbine in the opposite direction.

As a result, I was sent to the library after school, to spend an hour there contemplating my impertinence. A teacher called Mr. Whitely was supervising detention that day. Mr. Whitely had a beard and drove a Volkswagen Beetle. Mr. Whitely was . . . *different*. Normally, pupils in detention were expected to knuckle down and get on with some course-work. Mr. Whitely had other ideas. He would make you read for an hour. You were not allowed to read the book of *your* choice, however; you had to read the book of *Mr. Whitely's* choice. The book he selected for me had an image of two ladies in ball gowns on the cover. I laughed. I was four-teen. I loved soccer and the Beatles. I couldn't possibly read a book about women in ball gowns. I pushed it away. Mr. Whitely pushed it back. He tapped the cover. "Read," he said, without saying anything at all.

One hour later, Mr. Whitely returned to tell me I could go home. I was still reading. I was two pages from the end of a chapter. I asked Mr. Whitely if I could stay another ten minutes. Mr. Whitely raised an eyebrow. He looked around the library, perhaps to make certain that aliens had not invaded and replaced me with an exact book-loving replica. He said, "Take the book home and finish it." I shook my head. My friends would ridicule me if they saw me holding a book called . . . *Pride and Prejudice*. But Mr. Whitely was persuasive. So I took the book home and read it under the bedcovers, by flashlight. I enjoyed it. And when I returned it a week later, Mr. Whitely introduced me to more books, including one that would change my life. It was called *The Hobbit*. It had a dragon on the cover.

When people ask, "What's the best thing about being an author?" I tell them the story of Mr. Whitely, and how he opened a door in me that led to a world of infinite adventures, a door I've been striving to open for others ever since I began writing stories. Perhaps this is best summed up by a poignant letter I received years ago, from a mom who'd been reading *The Fire Within* with her son. She wrote, "My son is profoundly dyslexic. Until we found your book, he would not voluntarily read a menu! But because he was so caught up in the mystery, this is the first book he has attempted to read by himself. That is a miracle for him. Thank you." No, Mom. Thank Mr. Whitely. I think he would have been proud.

21. Reading shows you the woods and helps you through

by Jennifer Donnelly

When I was eight years old, I wanted the truth.

About life. People. The world.

But the grown-ups wouldn't give it to me.

Mr. Rogers didn't. Neither did Bert and Ernie, my parents, or my teachers. The nuns didn't. Nor did Scooby-Doo, Count Chocula, or President Nixon.

I wanted to know why Christmas carols made me feel sad. Why my tough-as-nails state trooper father sometimes cried. Why M&M's *did* melt in my hand.

Grown-ups think kids can't handle the truth. They want kids to feel safe and protected. To be happy. That's why they invented Batman and Santa and Cap'n Crunch. To show that things are fine, that someone's in charge and he's handing out prizes.

But kids sense there's more to the story. At night, lying on my stomach on the living room floor with my coloring books, I would listen as the somber voices on the television told my parents about Vietnam, Attica, Watergate.

I didn't understand body counts. Riots and tear gas. Or a president who lied. And no one explained them to me. The grown-ups were busy and tired and impatient. Now that I am one, I know they were also afraid.

And then, on a weekly trip to the library, I discovered a copy of *Grimm's Fairy Tales* and everything changed.

The Brothers Grimm were story collectors. They traveled around Germany, listened to folktales and fairy tales, and wrote down what they heard. And what they heard wasn't always pretty. Because life wasn't always pretty.

In the Grimms' version of "Hansel and Gretel," the kids don't just get lost in the woods. Their father abandons them there. Because their stepmother tells him to. They are poor and don't have enough to eat and if they can get rid of the kids, well . . . that's two less mouths to feed.

In the Grimms' "Cinderella," the ugly stepsisters are so desperate to marry the prince, they cut off pieces of their feet to fit into the glass slipper. They're ugly, we're told. What choice do they have?

I loved these stories. I still do. Because in them, the Grimms acknowledge something profound and essential—that the woods are real, and dark, and full of wolves. That I will, at times, get hopelessly lost in them. But they told me something else, too—that I can beat that darkness. Gretel was just a kid, but she beat the witch. Jack outran the giant. Red Riding Hood escaped from the wolf.

The brothers showed me that I am all I need, that I have all I need, to get out of the woods and find my way home. In their wild, weird, and wonderful fairy tales, I finally found the truth.

22. Reading lets you go to places and see things you never would or could

by Jenny Downham

I grew up in a house without books. My parents, both from working-class backgrounds, left school at fourteen and thought reading wasn't for people "like them."

I discovered stories at school. The teacher would read to the class at the end of each day, and on Friday, in assembly, the principal read to the entire school. But we weren't allowed to take books home and the nearest library was a long bus ride away.

When I was six, my cousin gave me a battered anthology he'd outgrown. It was called *Favourite Poems to Read Aloud*. I took this as an instruction and recited them constantly. I imagine this annoyed my mother, because for my next birthday I was given two books of my own: *Grimm's Fairy Tales* and *Legends from Ancient Greece*. "At least they'll keep you quiet," she said.

They utterly transported me. I'd never realized that could happen. They took me away from home and put me in other places. Not safe places, either. Scary and dangerous ones full of lost children and wicked adults and buckets of blood! There were no gauzy-winged fairies in Grimm, despite the title. As for ancient Greece—Pandora daring to disobey the gods and open the box entrusted to her care was the most terrifying and exciting story I'd ever read.

At mealtimes, I'd put my books down and force myself to journey home. I'd look at my family over the dinner table and think, *You've no idea where I've been* . . .

It wasn't until I went to a secondary school with a wonderful library that books became readily accessible. It was here that I borrowed Robert C. O'Brien's *Z for Zachariah*, a story about the end of the world. There's one survivor—a sixteen-year-old girl called Ann, who manages to keep living with grace and wisdom. I loved that book. It wasn't that I wanted to *be* Ann. I really didn't. But I wanted to know that she was possible—someone like her. She made me feel brave. Perhaps I was also capable of being such a person?

And here is my reason for reading—books let you go to places and see things you never would or could, or perhaps would want to in real life. You can meet protagonists who are able to tap into their own intelligence and resourcefulness. They might mess up, as we all do. They might go down the wrong path, or make terrible decisions, or feel afraid. They might have to ask advice or seek practical help, but you can watch them stumble and pick themselves up again and, as they grow and learn, so will you, walking beside them.

I feel sad that my mum never read a book in her life, never turned to a book for comfort or escape or guidance. But I feel blessed that she encouraged me to read, despite not understanding what I gained from it.

I explored safely, Mum, that's what. I received manageable doses of terror that produced antibodies (rather like a vaccine) to help me fight real-life fears.

Books are an easily accessible, extraordinary, and valuable resource. The story inside might give you strength, make you laugh, move you, make you think, feed you, stimulate your curiosity, and encourage you to ask questions of the world. It might scare you too, of course. But what if that gives you the courage to deal with a real-life challenge?

So, pick up a book—borrow one if you don't have any of your own—and begin a journey today.

23. Reading is a beautiful, scientific mystery

by Julie Falatko

When I talk to students about writing, I tell them that the process of being a writer is the same for me as it is for them. I struggle to get my ideas to be as great on the page as they are in my head. And then I revise. A lot.

All of that is true, but what I don't say is: I still don't get how it works. I am a writer. That's my actual job. But I don't know how writing and reading actually WORK. It's a scientific mystery.

I think of a scene. I write it down. And somehow, by doing that, a reader who is hundreds of miles away from me can see that scene I made up in their own head.

I can write a joke in my house in Maine and make someone in Texas laugh.

A book is flat letters on a page. The letters don't move. They don't dance or sing. But reading a book can make me smile. How? Do those marks on the pages transmit humor waves through the air into my brain and activate my smile muscles? It's probably that the ink in the letters diffuses ambient hilarity molecules into my brain hemispheres. Or maybe that the words pile into microscopic telepathic image transmission ships that fly into my ears.

Definitely one of those.

It has to be, because how else can some paper sewn into a cardboard cover make me smile if I'm reading out in public? That's amazing!

I remember the first book that made me cry, *Bridge to Terabithia* by Katherine Paterson. How dare this book make my cry? I couldn't believe it. But it did.

A book can let you literally read someone else's mind, because authors take things from their heads and write them down for you. All those words in books are describing someone else's thoughts. And if you read a lot of books, you're getting a lot of practice reading other people's minds (it's a scientific fact!). Maybe reading helps you read everyone's thoughts, not just the ones written down in books. I'm reading hundreds of books so I'll be able to read people's brains. I'll let you know how it goes.

I'm going to keep writing, and I'm going to keep reading. It's fun. But also, if I keep it up, one of these days I might crack the science of how squiggles can transform from words into feelings in my brain. I think it's either metamorphosis, photosynthesis, or magic.

24. Reading is a tool of freedom

by Sharon G. Flake

My great-grandmother didn't have much schooling. But she loved to read the Bible, and she loved her grandchildren. "Read anything—even if it's a comic book," she told them. My father took her wisdom to heart. As a result, we grew up in a home where reading wasn't just a priority. It was something done out of love.

Dad only made it to the eighth grade. At fifteen, he traveled north in the Colored section of the train along with his cousin and his grandmother's wisdom. He carried a cardboard suitcase. The fifty dollars in his pocket came from working construction at an army camp in North Carolina. He never formally furthered his education. But to this day, he is one of the most well-informed people I've ever known. If I want to know about World War 1, I call Dad. If I'm curious about which president ran against whom and when—I dial my father up. He's ninety-three now and his memory isn't as sharp, but he's still my go-to person for historical events, geographical wonders, and politics—local, national, *and* international.

Mom and Dad devoured newspapers. My five siblings and I can still recall running around the corner to the store to buy the *Daily News*. Back then, papers were as thick as hoagies. The Sunday paper was super wide as couch cushions. Our parents read the newspaper each day, from cover to cover. Midweek they purchased and read the African American newspaper—the *Tribune*. The papers went into the trash only after every word and idea had been gleaned and digested, it seemed.

My parents showed us by example that there was something important between those pages. I read about the Vietnam War, Martin's marches, Rizzo's raids. Sitting at the supper table, all eight of us would share our views about our community and the world. This was no quiet affair. We did a poor job at taking turns or listening to one another. Us kids especially were too filled up with what we'd read in the papers or learned from the evening news the night before to be polite.

We never heard our great-grandmother utter her infamous words. But we lived them nonetheless. My sister became a voracious reader. She loved high fashion magazines, the classics. Later in life, after traveling the world, she worked as a hospital aide. She'd find old copies of the *Financial Times* and the *Wall Street Journal,* and read them during her break. Doctors and strangers, she told us later, would stare as if she and those publications didn't match up. But my sister was doing exactly what she was raised to do—reading anything and everything that suited her fancy.

I wasn't like my sister or dad when it came to reading. I enjoyed reading. But I loved television. Still, I spent a fair share of time in libraries, toting home piles of books. Once, I borrowed one from a friend. Reading the evening away in a tub, I dropped the book in the water. Alone in the house, I placed it dripping wet into a hot oven. My hope was to restore it to its original state. But the pages curled and browned. The glue that held it together melted. Embarrassed, I paid my friend for the novel. I do not recall borrowing any more books from her. But the pleasure I get from reading remains. My great-grandmother's words do as well: "Read anything—even if it's a comic book." If we give young people this sort of freedom, perhaps they will exceed the limitations the world most surely will impose on them. Armed with such a tool, they too will discover new worlds, set their sights on whichever mountains they wish—and fly.

25. Reading gets you into the club

by Aimee Friedman

I still remember that day. I was in the fourth grade, waiting in line in the school cafeteria, when I overheard two students raving about a book series they loved called the Baby-sitters Club. It was about a group of girls who ran their own baby-sitting business, and all the dramas and victories that ensued. My ears perked up; I was a voracious reader, and always searching for new books to consume.

That evening, with my mom's blessing, I ordered the latest title in the Baby-sitters Club series—*#15: Little Miss Stonybrook . . . and Dawn*—off my Scholastic Book Club flyer. When the book arrived, with its bright and appealing illustrated cover, I dove in right away. And I was hooked. As soon as I finished, I ran to the library, and the bookstore, and anywhere I could get my hands on books 1–14. I caught up, and then waited breathlessly for the next installment.

Most of the novels I had read before were period pieces, or fantasies, or somber "classics" that my parents or teachers pressed on me. Nothing quite hit me where I lived like the Baby-sitters Club. The author, Ann M. Martin, wrote in a warm, familiar style that made the characters feel as real as any kids I knew. Kristy, Claudia, Stacey, Mary Anne, and Dawn talked and laughed and fought and dressed and dreamed just like my friends and I did. They dealt with homework and crushes and family strife. And I loved that they were, on balance, kind to each other. In my own life, and in some of the contemporary fiction I *had* read, a fair amount of cruelty between girls was somehow celebrated. What a gift it was to see young women being supportive of each other, and working their way through disagreements with empathy. There was conflict, to be sure—any good story will have that—and never any sort of preachy messaging (kids are allergic to such things). But ultimately the books provided a safe, cozy haven where friendship and sisterhood won the day.

Reading and writing were always my havens—my favorite activities, my constant companions. Like so many writers, I was a shy and sensitive kid, and I sought solace in stories. I'd been writing stories ever since I *could* write—around age five—but I began writing in earnest, filling up notebook after notebook, around the time I started reading the Baby-sitters Club. I think those books gave me the freedom—the permission—to write about the day-to-day lives of girls who might not have superpowers or wield swords, but instead worried about school and friends, and found empowerment through chasing their passions.

Without the Baby-sitters Club, I don't think I'd be the person (let alone the reader, writer, and editor) I am now. Does that sound like an exaggeration? Ask the countless BSC fans—both of my generation, and the readers still discovering the series today—and you'll find many who feel the same, and share their love for the books via articles and podcasts and adaptations. We've become our own club, and the bond we share is proof positive of just how powerful and inspiring books can be. BSC forever!

26. Reading is chocolate

by Cornelia Funke

We all, writers of stories, makers of books, know that not everyone likes to read them. In fact, most people don't—as so often books are forced on children like some kind of medicine, and we all know how that tastes!

Read this and you'll be a better person. Read this and you'll develop your writing skills. Read this and you'll get better grades.

Those of us who are lucky enough to love books nevertheless know of course that the medicine part should be ignored. No grown-up would walk into a bookstore and say: *Can you please suggest a book that makes me a better person? Or educates me on some painful truths?*

No.

We don't love books because they're good for us. (Although I do believe they are.) We love them because they can taste like chocolate, like foreign spices we never tasted before. We love them because they take us through magical wardrobes and to foreign planets. We love them because they open doors and windows when our world seems so small and gray. And those that are really good make us see that world far more clearly, in bright colors, all its mysteries and magic revealed.

Books make us into shape-shifters. They teach us to walk in somebody else's shoes and teach us how it feels to be hungry, happy, angry, tired, so afraid that we can barely move, so sad that we drown in our own tears . . . They teach us that it doesn't matter what color our skin has, whether we're boys or girls. They give us words for what we feel—when we believe that no one else feels that way! Books give us companions who understand when nobody else does, printed friends who are like us, when everyone seems so different.

Sometimes they even give us wings, the scales of a fish, the legs of a spider, or they show us how it may feel to be a tree. They can make us understand that life comes in many shapes on this planet and that we don't have to fear someone just because they look or talk different—or have fur.

And the adventures! All the dangers we dare to confront between the safe pages of a book. We still feel that courage when we put it back on a shelf, the strength it gave us to travel with its words. We can die and meet the death of others in a book. It can prepare us for all the hardship this life throws at us. And it is wonderful to meet loss or grief or heartbreak with the thought: hm, I remember when Hermione was jealous of Ron's girlfriend. I remember when that boy's best friend died . . . what was his name? Sometimes we may forget the title and the author of a book, but we won't forget how it made us feel. I've heard from dying children that they rode my dragons facing death; I heard from a female soldier that *Inkdeath* helped her survive a war. I heard from a girl who never had a family that she found one reading about the children in *Thief Lord*.

Yes. It's a magical task to write books. For they are printed shelters from the storm. And at the same time they hold all the words that do explain the storm.

So no! Don't ever sell them as medicine. They're chocolate. The best and richest chocolate in the world.

27. Reading gives you unexpected new friends

by Eric Gansworth

If you were born at the Tuscarora Indian Nation after 1900, you likely wouldn't have a loving relationship with books. I suspect this is true on many reservations. Books were associated with school, which terribly echoed the US government's systematic attempt to erase indigenous cultures: the Indian Boarding Schools. Many reservation households did not own books. Mostly, I saw books on library shelves, lining the lunchroom walls in our school.

In kindergarten, I enjoyed reading comics and monster magazines, but knew I was missing jokes aimed at an older audience. I mastered schoolbooks to improve my magazine comprehension skills. By third grade, I was placed with the fourth grade for reading period, and our assigned book was John Steinbeck's *The Red Pony*. The novel, set on a ranch, featured cowboys as major players. Though cowboys were scarce in upstate New York, where my reservation exists, I knew what they were. Tension between "cowboys and Indians" was a mainstay on TV, in movies, cartoons. In those places, Indians represented danger for the hero trailblazing cowboys. I wasn't eager to read this book that might paint me as a deterrent to "progress."

The complex style immediately attracted me and I began reading toward improving my skills. By the end of the second page, I'd glimpsed the cowboy Billy Buck and his world as a live-in ranch hand. Though connected intimately to his employers, the Tiflins, Billy actively displayed his employee status at all times. He was dressed, waiting, before Mrs. Tiflin rang the breakfast bell, but couldn't enter and join the meal until family members were ready. Young readers were supposed to identify with Jody, the adolescent main character, but I was drawn to Billy Buck's familiar practiced subservient position. I knew how to behave like him. My mother cleaned the houses of white people in the tony "village" near the reservation, and if I went along, I had to perform "subservient kid" behaviors so the homeowners felt safe with my presence.

I was fascinated witnessing the same dynamic playing out among these white characters. I wanted to inhabit their world, desperately longed to ask Billy Buck what his life was like. Because of my mother's jobs, I'd understood that white people around us considered us "lesser," but on the Rez, we had each other, a community. I wondered how Billy Buck navigated being "lesser" among his own. It never even occurred to me that I should question why *we* existed in that place. I'd been prone to empathy from a very early age, for animals, people, and TV characters—more than was acceptable, truthfully. I tried to share the good news about the magic of books and the characters you could grow to love. I told a sibling I wanted to meet Billy Buck.

"Don't say ridiculous things like that out loud! People *already* think you're too weird," my sibling said. The walled-off emotional states the boarding schools had instilled in us through our grandparents rose up and punched me in the face again. You learned quickly what not to do when it flared. We lived in a hard world and I'd already learned how to thrive inside my head.

I was sad I didn't have the skills to share this joy, but fortunately, reading is a quiet, private activity I could enjoy on my own. I discovered that books offered alternative worlds, sometimes worlds as harsh as mine, where things were never as simple as they seemed. That understanding made my own life less lonely and set me on the lifelong path to a world lined with books, each filled with another potential friend.

28. Reading works on your mind

by Lamar Giles

My mom had a plan.

See, she was a factory employee in a factory town, happy to have the work. But she'd be the first to tell you it was hard physical labor done around really dangerous machinery. Safety regulations didn't mean she was safe. At all. Even if you avoided daily injuries (like she mostly did), long-term effects on the body were inevitable. Life in "the plant" was not the sort she wanted for her children. Often, she'd tell me and my sister, "Work on your mind, because if you work on your mind when it's your turn to go out into the world and make a living for yourself, at the very least you can have air-conditioning."

How does one work on their mind? According to Mom, books. My sister and I would argue the answer was toys, but we lost that one more often than not. Shopping trips became this compromise (or bribe, depending on how you looked at it) where we were definitely not getting a toy, BUT if we found a book we wanted, we could have it. Every time.

There were some problems with this approach. Those trips were often to the meager grocery store in our factory town, where the book section was five shelves the width of a refrigerator. The children's books that were available weren't the most appealing, yet, since books were the only option for acquisition, I was determined to always find something I could take home. This was the reason I read *Misery* by Stephen King around age eight (not recommended).

The other problem: Having set the precedent of always saying yes to a book, shopping trips became more expensive in a way Mom hadn't anticipated. She couldn't retract the offer—that wouldn't be encouraging the sharpening of our minds, now would it?—but she couldn't go broke over it, either. The most obvious solution presented itself in the squat brick building a block away from the grocery store: the public library.

We could still take books home (albeit temporarily) but we were no longer limited by the paltry selection of a store that specialized in quality cuts of meat. We could check out something like twenty books if we wanted. For free (provided we returned them before the due date). There was a whole children's section . . . though I still checked out books way beyond my years. I read *The Dark Half* by Stephen King at age nine (again, not recommended). And while toys still held some appeal—I was a Teenage Mutant Ninja Turtles guy—our tastes began to skew toward the unique portal magic that only books provided. Time travel and space adventures through science fiction. The magical kingdoms of fantasy. Mom's plan worked—and as we know, history repeats itself.

My sister's got her son, my nephew, on the same always-say-yes-to-a-book plan. I write books, so my words are making it to the hands of eager kids working on their minds. Mom made a lot of things in that factory, but outside it was where she forged her rarest creations: a couple of readers. Now we're self-replicating!

29. Reading can give you words to help you know and name yourself

by Alex Gino

I first read the word *genderqueer* in Kate Bornstein's *Gender Outlaws: On Men, Women, and the Rest of Us* when I was nineteen. Finding a word to describe people who don't connect with either the gender they were assigned at birth or the "opposite" gender was like finding out I existed. I consumed the word and concept that I had been needing for so long like I'd had a vitamin deficiency. I ate it right up, nom nom nom. It became part of my bones and my flesh, and with it, I was able to better piece together who I was and am.

While I was delighted to find myself in Auntie Kate's words, and my endless thanks to her for that, I was indignant that no one had ever bothered to tell me there was a *rest of us* before, those of us who aren't male or female. Of course, they most likely didn't know themselves. I love reading because it can help us figure out who we are, even when the people around us won't or can't. The people and ideas we read about can be models for our own lives that we haven't found elsewhere.

This is especially important for young LGBTQIAP+ (Lesbian Gay Bisexual Transgender Queer Intersex Asexual Pansexual +) folks, who are often the only queer and/or trans person (that they know of) in their family. And while more kids are coming out, there are still plenty of young folk who don't have queer or trans friends (again, that they know of). Without queer and trans elders and peers, reflections are rare. Books are a way that we know our feelings are real—that *we* are real. And that's not at all limited to nonfiction. Fiction is a wealth of opportunity for reflections. The characters and events may not be factual, but they ring with truth and connection, and reading about people like us can help us feel real ourselves.

I've heard from kids (and adults) who tell me that Melissa, the main character of my book *George*, is the first trans person that they've ever known, outside of themselves. I'm reminded in particular of a young person who I met twice. The first time was when she first held Melissa's story. The second time, she asked me to sign a copy to her new name. In those six months, she met Melissa and was able to come out as trans and name herself. I can't imagine my words having a more important effect on a person.

Of course, books aren't the only way LGBTQIAP+ kids and other marginalized folks find connection. More and more young queer and trans kids have queer and trans friends and peers, and rainbow alliance—type groups are becoming more common in high schools, middle schools, and, yes, elementary schools. I am heartened by the knowledge that kids like I was are now seeing themselves as a part of literature, and thus, a part of society. For those kids, sharing and talking about queer books and stories is an invaluable bonding experience and an opportunity to explore what connects us as well as what makes us unique.

Note that I use the word *genderqueer* above. In the story of my life, that's the word where I feel most at home. If I were reading what's available today, I might well have connected with the word *nonbinary*. The fact that we each have our own reaction to what we read, based on who we are and what we've faced, is just another thing to love about reading. Particularly in queer communities, language is rapidly morphing as we grow in response to long-denied freedoms. And I'm excited to keep reading to learn language and concepts that account for who we are and where we're going.

30. Reading builds bridges

by Christina Diaz Gonzalez

Books as bridges. It wasn't something I'd often considered, but as I think more on the topic, I see how books have often been an important connection in introducing me to new people or places. When I was young, books were a link that could transport me to fantastic faraway lands or provide me with a hidden insight into a story that hit closer to home. Books were my companions, and I took them everywhere. I especially remember sitting in my tree house, reading and getting lost in stories filled with action and adventure. Hours would go by and yet time seemed to stand still.

Perhaps this fragmenting of time and place made books such as *A Wrinkle in Time* such a clear favorite for a young Latina girl growing up in the Deep South. I loved the chance to explore new worlds and meet new people, which in turn gave me the opportunity to learn more about myself within the safety of the pages of the book. Being an avid reader prompted me to search for stories that might reflect my own experience of living a bicultural life, but, unfortunately, finding those types of books was nearly an impossible task during that time. Thankfully, today's readers have more (but not nearly enough) diverse books, which are exceptionally important, as they not only serve to validate diverse experiences, but they also allow a reader to see the familiar inside the foreign. It is this power found within books that gives us insight into another's experience.

And this power found in reading can also create a special link between books and our own memories by establishing a bridge that can transcend time itself. When that connection is formed, a book ceases to be an inanimate object sitting on a shelf and instead becomes part of who we are. For me, this happens when I allow myself to think back to a favorite moment, such as the days I spent reading to my grandmother. If I close my eyes, I can travel back through time to when I was a young girl and I would be sitting in her room, on her flowered bedspread, where she would ask me to read Spanish magazines to her. I remember being amazed at stories of royal families living in Europe and comparing them to the fairy tales I had read in English. In retrospect, it was all an obvious plot by my abuela to ensure that I learned how to read in Spanish, but there was also something quite magical about sharing those moments reading together. It was a connection between cultures, between generations, and between languages. Even now, after so many years have passed, whenever I see those Spanish magazines, a bridge seems to cross over the chasm of time, and I'm able to briefly relive those moments with my abuela once again.

So, I ask you to cross your own divide and think of those favorite books or reading moments as vehicles that can help take you to a different time and place. Consider the real-life people who played a part in your own reading adventures . . . an encouraging teacher, a comforting parent reading to you at bedtime, or perhaps your own abuelita who lovingly gazed at you as you mangled several words in another language . . . these are the people who you can revisit, even if only as a memory, when books become imprinted in your heart and mind. You see, books can truly be the most magical of bridges.

31. Reading takes you and your fears seriously

by Alan Gratz

When I was a kid, I was terrified of dying.

I was afraid of dying in a general sense: I didn't want to be gone forever from the world. I really, really liked life (I still do!) and I didn't want to *not* be living anymore. Call it the world's biggest case of FOMO ever.

But I was also specifically afraid of dying while I was asleep. I was so afraid of dying in my sleep that I would stay awake as long as I could every night. My parents would come into my room and say, "Alan, go to sleep!" I would say, "I can't! I'm afraid I'll die while I'm sleeping!" and my parents would say, "You're not going to die. Go to sleep." My parents didn't understand. It may have been very silly to think I was going to die in my sleep, but to me, at age eight, nine, ten, the fear was very real.

I was scared to death of dying.

Then, in seventh grade, my class read a book called *Tuck Everlasting* by Natalie Babbitt. In *Tuck Everlasting*, a family drinks from a magic spring and lives forever. They never die.

It sounded great to me. I didn't ever want to die! I wanted to live forever! But the Tucks come to realize that maybe living forever isn't such a good thing after all. At its heart, *Tuck Everlasting* is about how growing old and dying is a natural and essential part of the cycle of life.

I was stunned. Here was a book written for kids my age—in seventh grade!—that fixated on death as much as I did. That said to me, "I get it. Death is scary. Let's talk about it." *Tuck Everlasting* didn't change my mind about death. When I was done reading it, I still wanted to live forever. But for the first time, I felt like an adult was taking me and my very real, very specific fears seriously. I felt seen.

When I became an author, I wanted to write books that did the same thing. All my books are exciting, fast reads, but they tackle tough stuff too. *Prisoner B-3087* is a hard, honest look at what life was like for a boy in the Holocaust. *Code of Honor* shows how people of Middle Eastern descent experience prejudice in the United States post-9/11. *Projekt 1065* examines what it takes for a kid who was bullied to become a bully himself. *Refugee* shows the difficult, dangerous journey refugees face when they are driven from their homes by violence. *Grenade* examines the horrors of war, particularly for the people caught in the middle. *Allies* asks how we can continue to discriminate against people who aren't like us when it is so very clear that we can get more done and be stronger and better when we work together.

I write about tough stuff because I know, like Natalie Babbitt did, that young readers can handle it. I know you have questions about the world, about life, just like I did, and I want to talk about those things as honestly and thoughtfully as she did. I may not have all the answers—and even if I think I do, I may not change your mind. But I will always write books that take you seriously. I promise.

Oh, and I still don't want to die. If you're reading this, and think someday you might become a medical researcher who cures death, I would appreciate you getting on that sooner rather than later.

32. Reading gives you an escape . . . and a home

by Melissa Grey

There's a phrase in Latin that literally means "go with me." *Vade mecum.* It refers to that one book you can't live without. That one book that "goes with you." Growing up, that book for me was *From the Mixed-Up Files of Mrs. Basil E. Frankweiler.* I carried my dingy, dog-eared copy with me everywhere. Between its pages, I both lost and found myself.

You see, I had an unhappy childhood. My home never quite felt like a safe space. So reading about children who made their own home in a place as magical as the Metropolitan Museum of Art was inspirational to me. I formed all these grand plans about doing what Claudia and Jamie Kincaid did; I would save up all the loose change I could scrounge up in my couch cushions and make my own life somewhere else. I even lived in New York City! The Metropolitan Museum was right there!

But sadly, on a school trip to that very same museum, I found that the Met, with its security guards and all-seeing cameras, wasn't nearly as receptive to overnight guests as E.L. Konigsburg would have me believe. I would never pluck spare change out of the fountain to do my laundry and buy vending machine dinners. I would never sleep in Napoleon III's bed. I learned that life could not always imitate art. I couldn't escape my life the way the Kincaid children had. But what the book did teach me was that I *could* escape. It was just a different kind of escape, unlimited by the constraints of reality.

Books were my escape.

And I wasn't limited to just one. Every book was its own world, its own universe. Each one had its own rules and brave heroes breaking those rules. I could lose myself in Tolkien's Middle-earth or Mercedes Lackey's Valdemar or J.K. Rowling's Hogwarts. Fiction made all things possible. And if those incredible authors could create such vivid and wonderful worlds . . . then maybe I could too.

I knew then that my *vade mecum*—the book that "went with me" always—hadn't led me astray. It had led me home.

While I couldn't live in the Metropolitan Museum of Art, I basically did live in an equally important institution: the library. (Though they didn't let me sleep there either.) And no library had a greater impact on me than the New York Public Library's main branch on Fifth Avenue. It's a beautiful old building guarded by two majestic stone lions. It is grand and opulent and full of the most important things in my world: books. *This* was where I belonged. And this was where I would write my first book (and where the heroine of that book would live as a runaway child).

And now, every time I sit down to write a new book, I remember the way *From the Mixed-Up Files of Mrs. Basil E. Frankweiler* made me feel. And if I manage to make even one reader feel that way, then I'll know I've done what I've set out to do.

33. Reading is of enormous importance

by Virginia Hamilton

Literature, like justice, begins on a simple, human level. Such as paying attention, listening, answering questions, seeing the problems, and sensing that our understanding, our kindness, serves a good purpose.

I had a friend, Danny, who some years ago was in elementary school with my son. Danny was very proud of me. He didn't know much about my relationship to the world, but in my hometown I received a lot of attention, and he knew I must be somebody. Since he was in class with my son, Jaime, and they were friends, then he was somebody, too. Danny would sometimes come home with Jaime and he would take time to visit with me. Clearly I had become one of his favorite attractions—the somebody. But then I believe his concept of me changed, to puzzled curiosity about what I did, the making of books. We talked about that one day. I told him that a book had to have a start and a finish. And in between, there had to be something going on, something that would hold the reader there inside the book. "You have to mess around in there and keep things going," I told him.

"You mean like a fight?" he asked.

"Maybe a fight," I answered. "At least, you have to have folks doing things that get them upset and confused and maybe trying things out on one another sometimes."

"You can do that?" Danny wanted to know.

"I can do anything I want to the folks in my books," I said, "and nobody can stop me."

Well, he thought about that. "You're the boss in there," he said. I could tell he liked that. But I was aware he wanted to ask me something very important to him and was having a hard time. Danny stared at me a long time before he finally blurted it out: "But where do you get all those different words?" he asked. Well, I was speechless for a moment before I realized that Danny probably had never read a book. And he thought a book was full of words, no two of which were the same. Think of that; think of the fear in Danny, defeating himself, creating failure before he'd even started.

I informed him that I used almost all the same words over and over again in every book. "I don't learn a whole volume of new words each time I write," I said. "For example," I told him, "I use *the*, *is*, *it*, *he*, *she*, *open*, *close*, *inside*, *outside*, *grass*, *car*, *tree*, *sky* hundreds of times in books. I only know a certain number of words."

Telling him that seemed to make things a lot easier for him.

But isn't it curious what young people imagine when they are afraid? And yet, although my young friend wasn't a reader, somewhere along the way he understood the importance of books and reading.

I talk to many young people in and outside of this country, young people from age seven or eight to sixteen and seventeen, and I have never spoken to one of any age who did not know somewhere inside that books and reading and writing were of enormous importance. Even those who weren't readers knew how important reading was.

This selection was adapted from Virginia Hamilton's 1990 commencement address at Bank Street College. © 2020 The Arnold Adoff Revocable Living Trust. Used By Permission.

34. Reading will keep you company

by Karen Hesse

In 1961 I ran away from home. I was nine years old. I was certain my parents didn't love me, and I needed to figure out how to proceed with the rest of my life. The place I ran to was my local library, a favorite destination for as long as I could remember. I loved my neighborhood library; I felt safe there.

I'd never come on my own before. Usually my brother walked me there.

Unaccompanied, in that big, light-filled building, I felt very small and vulnerable, but also very grown-up and powerful.

My plan was to stay at the library for the rest of my life. There was a bathroom where I could wash up. I didn't eat much so I didn't worry about food. And there were books, enough books to last a lifetime.

When I didn't show up for dinner that evening, my mother sent my brother out looking for me.

It didn't take him long to find me.

I rejoiced at seeing him when he first joined me at the round library table.

But then he spoke.

"You are in big trouble," he said.

"I don't care," I told him. "I'm never going home."

My brother was sympathetic but firm.

I was stubborn but also a little scared.

The library was preparing to close for the day. The children's librarian, who I adored, had been monitoring my presence all afternoon and was too wise to be fooled if I'd tried ducking into the bathroom to hide until the doors were locked.

So I finally swallowed my pride and allowed my brother to lead me out the big glass doors and back home.

I'd entered the library hours earlier, empty-handed, carrying with me only my seething temper.

I departed the library with an armful of newly borrowed books.

Ever since cracking the reading code in first grade, I'd discovered that reading, more than most anything else, filled me with delight and wonder, challenged me to think, and feel, and grow. To walk in other people's shoes. Books helped me escape a difficult childhood made even more difficult by my own pigheaded, prickly self. The isolation I felt in my heart was temporarily eased by the companions I traveled with in books. I had problems. They had problems. I read carefully to see how their dilemmas resolved. Then I integrated their experiences into my own. It took me years to develop a personal ethic unique to me. In the meantime I took inspiration from fictional (and occasionally real) characters.

I don't remember what happened to me when my brother and I returned home that evening. I don't think I got dinner that night. But I didn't eat much anyway, so that didn't feel like too great a punishment.

I'm pretty sure I was sent straight to my room.

But I had a stack of newly borrowed library books under my arm; a crowd of new friends waiting to keep me company. They would help me figure things out.

35. Reading gives you unexpected role models

by Tanuja Desai Hidier

Once upon a town
(1970s; Snow White)
American Dream–bound
Brown family arrives

Mom-ji hums Hindi songs
Lures fairies *Aai paree*
Saris stash starlight
Shelved beneath Levi jeans

BapuDad-ji prays in kitchen
Masala-brewing tea
Cupboard temples Lord Krishna
(Of its door relieved)

Children curl up in cursive
(Fingers stained PBJ)
Blue airmail *miss you* missives
From/to Grandpamas/Bombay

Lovingly these Little Housers
Look upon each other
But on TV screen, bookshelf, street?
Look unlike any other . . .

Recess stress: the girl ducks
Strenuously does not cry
Kevin her skin dog-doo dubbed
Flung sand into her eyes

Cherokee? Apache-hee?
One adult even taunted
Notes passed twitch: *Must be witch*
Was she? trembled she, haunted

Powww!

Piercing her brown skin
Raw arrow of shame
(Blood red in her vein;
Bonedeep, we're the same)

She begins to view brown
As embarrassing, dirt
A tincture of splintering
True hue of hurt

World wobbles, a puzzle
Her own map: in bits
India's elephant-trunk triangle
Just doesn't fit

Yet both severed parts
Beat in her heart
How to bring them together
And not fall apart?

Not "Indian" enough
Not "American" either
Census (brow lifts): Other
Here-or-there? Nor-n-neither

O! Somewhere a place

Broke things go to grow whole?
She wonders—discovers . . .

YES!
Just down the road!

Its code word: *library*—
Wilbraham, Mass girl's no fool:
T'was the Yellow Brick Road!
Super(wo)man's booth!

20,000 Leagues
Deep in stories she dives
Out the LionWitchWardrobe
Into magical lives . . .

One day stumbling upon
Villa Villekulla
Where a wonderkid heroine
How-do-you-do's her

Pippilotta Delicatessa Windowshade . . .
Longstocking
Aka: Pippi
(Who'll provide a pep-talking)

Fiery braids sticking out
Either side of her head
Pippi lives in this magical house . . .
By *herself*!

Brown girl (black braids down)
Lost in the page, found

Words swirling her worlds
Toward common ground

Pippi's privy to plural
Heartlands on a map:
Sweden, Seven Seas
(And's unafraid to own that)

She too for her difference:
Beleaguered, teased
Craycarroty hair
Freakfreckspeckled cheeks

Yet . . .

Never once does she doubt her self-
Love and -belief

To a shop clerk selling salve for
Freckles, to hide them
Pippi declares she *loves* them—
Requests one to *multiply* them!

Pippi stood up for herself
The child on the street
Aaray waah!—was she strong!
Could lift a horse from its feet

And she reached rightupoffathat page—
Lifted *me*
(As books do:
Into . . .
We)

A persona pluttifikate
(Her term for times tables):
Grit + Wit incarnate
Willing x Able

Herself unabashedly
x Infinity
Larger-than-life-largessely
Pippi thumbs-up-decreed:

If I can be so =
So YOU can be

Who was I to certify
Brown *dirt* (as in dirty?)
When it was tawn-bronze-dawn . . .
Earth? (Nth-degree worthy?)

I too—like YOU!—could be
Hero of my story
Lift up others, me, you—in truth:
It's my dharma, my duty!

I too could give more
Do utbest to ensure
Heroes in my home were
Seen in their bravery. Bounty. Beauty.

Years on I wrote an Indian-
American coming of age
Built my own Villa Villekulla
On *and* off the page . . .

Pippi hearing me, cheering me on all the way.

You don't have to fit labels
A box: us or them
Either/or. We're much *more*:
Galoreiously *and/and*!

A hyphen's not a border
It's also a bridge
The power of our stories
Pauses not on the page

Born by you
Bounds to the world . . .
Transforms you—
And you: the *universe*!

We can *imagine*
Speak, hear, write
READ our dreams
Into being

On a bookshelf
Find our true selves
Happy ends
And beginnings

And in a Pippi Longstocking
Make a forever friend

36.

READING BRINGS FAMILIES TOGETHER

BY JENNIFER L. HOLM & MATTHEW HOLM

> My little brother (Matt) is six years younger than me. Growing up, we didn't have a lot in common— but we both loved reading!

I never let anything get in the way of a good book. Not even chores!

Matt liked books so much he would hang out **ON** the bookshelf!

(Brothers are so weird.)

> Our shared love of reading brought us together in all sorts of places!

37. Reading helps us realize that everyone's story matters

by Deborah Hopkinson

If you were to meet me at an author visit, you'd probably notice right away that I'm short. Very short. I think most third graders are taller.

Actually, it's been that way since kindergarten. I was clumsy too. And really, REALLY horrible at sports. Back then (a long time ago), all we did for PE was play kickball on our asphalt school playground. Guess who was always picked last?

To make matters worse, the thing I *was* good at seemed like the wrong one: winning spelling bees. Once, after a classmate named David beat me in a spelling bee, he fell right over in a pretend faint. SLAM! He made everyone laugh and applaud. But no one wants to clap for the kid who wins all the time.

Truth is, I spent most of my time in school feeling embarrassed, awkward, and shy; I was unpopular and different. You can probably guess what I'm about to say next: I turned to reading.

From the time I was in fourth grade, I read constantly. I loved being transported by a story. But I also liked reading about real people and events. And the more I read, the more curious I got.

As I grew up, I started to notice there weren't many books about girls or ordinary people in history. I lived in a historic town (Lowell, Massachusetts), where in the 1800s girls and women had come from farms to work in some of America's first factories.

The deserted textile factories were still there, and I walked by them every day on my way to high school. I wondered: What if I had lived back then? What would it have been like to stand for fourteen hours a day running a loom? Would I have ever had a chance to read?

The stories of the Lowell mill girls weren't in my history books. Neither were the stories of enslaved people who'd been kidnapped and forced to work on cotton plantations in the South—the same cotton that was made into cloth in Lowell factories. Where were their stories?

Those questions started a lifelong learning journey. Books have helped me learn more about the past, along with talking with people, visiting museums, and traveling to places to see history with my own eyes. I've learned about the *Titanic*, World War II, the Holocaust, and the lives of immigrants. Reading nonfiction has helped me connect with people of the past, though I realize I can never truly know what their lives were like.

Once, after I became a writer, I was invited back to my high school and given an alumni award. In my speech, I quoted an immigrant factory worker whose oral history I'd found. She had a tremendous, determined spirit. Her story had moved me, and I included it in my Scholastic nonfiction book *Up Before Daybreak: Cotton and People in America*—a book that helped me answer some of the questions I'd had growing up.

When I finished, an elderly gentleman came up to me. "That woman you talked about was my mother," he said. "Thank you for sharing her story with others." (Today, visitors can also learn about the lives of factory workers at the Lowell National Historical Park.)

That's what reading nonfiction does: It connects us.

I hope you will read true stories of the past—collect stories from your family members. Don't forget to write your own story too. Because everyone's story matters.

Oh, and in case you're wondering, even though I didn't get taller, things did get better. Today, whenever I'm not reading or writing, I'm working out at the gym. But still no team sports.

38. Reading introduces you to lifelong friends

by Alaya Dawn Johnson

The friends I remember best from my childhood lived strange, adventure-filled lives. They suffered and fought but also danced before bonfires beneath the light of twin moons, ran along the eternally sunlit inner curve of a hollow planet, hunted dragons and learned swordcraft, and stood up to evil even though sometimes—even for them—it wasn't enough. Their names were Vesper, Mary, Justice, Alanna, Sirius, Aerin, Elsha, Lyra and Will, Meg and Charles Wallace, Anne, Kate, Sophie and Howl.*

They were funny and intrepid and sensible and brilliant and sometimes tremendously foolhardy. I loved them, fellow reader; I loved them as fiercely as only one of our tribe can. I loved Mary Lennox, the sour child who, after the destruction of her harsh, unloving home, is shipped with perfect indifference to a new one. I marveled alongside her slow awakening to the possibilities of magic in the everyday world. I wrote to myself, *Never stop believing in magic, Alaya.* A desperate warning from a trapped child to an adult she couldn't imagine. I never did stop. How could I? My friends held the magic for me, even when I was at my lowest. Lyra and Will and Elsha told me you could fight for better worlds. Aerin told me to push past bitterness and exhaustion, to keep trying for what I knew I needed. Sophie and Kate taught me to plan (and encouraged me to not let the clothes pile quite so high). Anne reminded me to write. My books held that door open for me; eventually, they helped me escape. I

---

*From, in order: The Vesper Holly series by Lloyd Alexander, *The Secret Garden* by Frances Hodgson Burnett, the Justice trilogy by Virginia Hamilton, the Lioness Quartet by Tamora Pierce, *Dogsbody* by Diana Wynne Jones, *The Hero and the Crown* by Robin McKinley, *Winter of Fire* by Sherryl Jordan, the His Dark Materials trilogy by Philip Pullman, *A Wind in the Door* by Madeleine L'Engle, *Anne of Green Gables* by L. M. Montgomery, *The Perilous Gard* by Elizabeth Marie Pope, and *Howl's Moving Castle* by Diana Wynne Jones.

had friends outside my books, thankfully, but they never knew—I never told them—all the worlds I had inside me.

As an adult, I am grateful to these childhood friends—though perhaps I could never be so grateful as that child I was, painstakingly deciphering alongside them a map of how to be her own hero. Now I can return to those old, familiar friends, and they spring to life as vibrantly as ever. They have not changed as I have, but that's part of the joy. I see new facets of what made me love them. I recognize bits of my own history in their disasters and their joys.

I am who I am today because these friends met me at the junction between dry page and living imagination; they gave the gift of recognition, that light in the dark, to a girl who needed it—and yes, that is a magic I will always believe in.

39. Reading can give you the past, present, and future

by Varian Johnson

When I was growing up, it often seemed like the only time I truly saw books about kids like me was in February—during Black History Month. While I relished the opportunity to pick up these books, I wasn't always happy with the choices, because they all seemed to be about slavery. About civil rights. About the struggle—*the burden*—of being black.

Don't get me wrong—these books are important. They have a vital place in our collections, and in our homes. Kids—and adults—need to read them. These books tell the story of those who have come before us.

But kids of color deserve a wide variety of stories. Serious books and historical books . . . but also funny books. Adventures. Mysteries. Stories where the boy with the brown skin saves the day, or the girl with the hijab solves the case.

That is why I am so excited about the state of publishing today. There are so many more book choices than when I was a kid. Today, we not only get to revisit our past in books, but we get to experience the present—and even the future! To not just exist in the book, but to be the hero. The star. And isn't that one of the most joyful things about reading a book . . . being able to see ourselves today, and being able to see the person we hope to be?

40. Reading changes gravity

by Jess Keating

Every time I open a book, I think of gravity on the moon. Because of gravity, the average African elephant weighs around 12,000 pounds here on Earth. Blue whales are even heavier—in fact, blue whales are thought to be the largest animal to have *ever* lived—at a whopping 130 tons or more. (If you're curious, that's as much as 25 elephants!)

But on the moon? Gravity doesn't play by the same rules. You could take a one-hundred-pound bag of candy to the moon and it would only weigh about seventeen pounds. Your heavy bag of candy would somehow be easier to carry. It sounds impossible, doesn't it? But it's science. We can use a fancy equation to explain why the moon's gravity makes things lighter.

That's why I love reading: Just like the moon, reading changes gravity. And by changing gravity, books let us do impossible things. All the rules are broken, and suddenly we're capable of carrying *anything*.

Does carrying everything you love sound impossible? It is. *Except* when you read.

With books, you can carry anything that piques your curiosity—whether it's whales or bunnies or mockingjays or impossibly big red dogs named Clifford. The world is yours! And the best part? Whatever you read is yours for life. You get to keep it, tucked away safely in your heart with everything else that has ever mattered to you. When you read, there is no limit to what you can carry. The rules of gravity no longer matter. Instead, magic takes their place.

Because, dear reader—reading *is* magic. There is no equation or calculation I can show you that explains how we can carry with us every book we've ever loved. Whether it's a story, a beloved friend, a comfort, a thrill, an escape, or an entire universe, reading allows you to defy gravity and carry these moments and experiences with you. Books change you because you carry their contents for the rest of your life.

The funny thing about books is that you'd never suspect them of magic like this. They all look pretty much the same, don't they? A spine. Two covers. Some pages in between with dark scribbles on them. Maybe a picture or two if you're lucky. In our world, we have rules about what's possible and impossible, but books are how we break those rules. Books let us sneak a little magic into our lives.

Never forget that you can do impossible things—as often as you like. You can read minds, you can go anywhere imaginable without any restrictions, and you can carry universes without breaking a sweat. And if someone asks where you heard such an impossible thing, you can tell them the truth: *You read it in a book.*

So when you look up at the moon on a quiet night before bed, think about where you'd like to go next, and what you'd like to carry with you on your journey through life. Seek out everything you love. Big things. Small things. Real things. Magical things. It's impossible, but you can carry them all.

Read.

Explore.

Then read some more.

41. Reading is like dancing with words

by Christine Kendall

The Literacy Day people were right in their guess that music and snacks would draw more folks to the book festival. I sat behind the two neat piles of books at my table, inhaled the buttery smell of popcorn, and watched a woman let herself go over at the DJ's booth—all shoulders and swinging hips. She pranced from one author's table to the next, picking up books and tucking them under her right arm so she was already loaded up pretty good when she got to me. I wondered for a moment if she could manage to browse through my book with her one free hand, but I'd already seen how this woman moved. She had good balance.

"I'd like to write," the woman said, flipping through my book, "but I don't have enough words."

Now, that already sounded like a poem to me.

"You have all the words you need," I said. "I know 'cause I saw you dancing over there."

That woman's eyes lit up like somebody had just given her free tickets to a dance-off.

"You think so?" she said.

"No doubt about it." I dropped my hands to my sides and stood stock still. "Something came over me." I recited those simple words that make up the opening sentence of a short story by Toni Cade Bambara. "You have those words," I said to the woman. "We all do."

I ran my hand over the smooth cover of my book and thought about what makes reading magical. It's the words, for sure, but it's not how many words a writer has. It's how we use words to get under the skin of our characters and bring their stories to life. It's empathy, the ability to share the feelings of others or, put another way, to feel their music. That's what's magical about reading and it's why I write. It's like dancing with words.

I looked over at the barbershop across the corner from where we were standing and saw a handsome teen bop down the steps, plop his baseball cap backwards on his newly shorn head, and turn our way. He slid across the street like he was walking on butter, but every move he made was in time to the DJ's beat. I don't think he knew the dancing woman, but they both lip-synced the song with flair, adding their own creative interpretation to the music.

The woman took her stack of books and moved on from my table. I imagined her putting her words down on paper to capture the rhythm of this neighborhood. A story just waiting to be told.

42. Reading is something that can be shared out loud

by Kody Keplinger

When I was nine years old, I brought home my first Harry Potter book. It seemed so thick to me, with way too many pages in way too small font. With my visual impairment, I'd have to read it with a magnifier, which seemed like such an impossibly daunting task. Luckily, I'd brought it home from the library that day because my mom had told me to, insisting that she wanted to see what all the hype was about (the first movie would be out soon) and that we could read it together.

Reading that book—and the next couple in the series—with my mom is one of my fondest childhood memories. Not just because of the books, though they became instant favorites, but because of the experience. I loved sitting on the couch, listening to her read, pausing to comment or gasp or share our intense emotions about a big moment in the story. But it didn't end with Harry Potter. We kept reading books together all the way through middle school and high school, and even to this day, sometimes when my mom visits, we pick a book for her to read aloud to me.

Being read aloud to is no longer a necessity in my life. Audiobooks and other accessible options have made reading solo much more feasible. Instead, we do it because it's fun. Because it's a way to bond—to share an experience that otherwise would be a solitary, isolated one.

My mom isn't the only person I've bonded with through read-aloud sessions, either. When I was in college, my roommate and I both shared a passion for young adult novels. When she learned I hadn't read a favorite book of hers, I tentatively made a suggestion: "Maybe we could read it together?" To my surprise and delight, she jumped at this. And from then on, every single night, right before bed, we'd kick out any other friends we had in our dorm room and read the next chapter or two of a novel.

This ended up being crucial for our budding friendship. It was a time of day when, no matter what else was going on in our lives, no matter what arguments we'd had or what homework was stressing us out, we put it aside and just engaged in a story together. She'd read, I'd listen, and we'd have something to discuss the next day. That was nearly a decade ago, and to this day, when my freshman-year roommate and I see each other, we still talk about some of the books we read together.

I love reading for the ways it can bring people together. Not just through fandom—though that's something I've always appreciated, too—but through the actual shared experience. There's something very intimate about being read to or reading to someone else. It's something I think we leave behind us in our childhood far too often. And I'm glad I've been lucky enough to have people in my life, even now in my late twenties, willing to sit down and read aloud with me.

Books can create bonds between us. Bonds that last a lifetime. And while I love reading a book by myself from time to time, I think the closeness I developed with my mom and my friends through shared reading experiences might be the biggest reason I love reading, and I am forever grateful for them.

43. Reading makes you the best kind of snoop

by Barbara Kerley

I've always been a people watcher. To be honest, I'm a bit of a snoop. I'm very interested in what other people are up to.

My husband and daughter think I ask *way* too many questions, but I can't help it. I find people fascinating. I want to know what they think is important, and why.

As a kid, I loved listening to stories about people who did extraordinary things—artists, scientists, explorers, and trailblazers of all kinds. I wanted to know everything I could about their lives. How did they achieve their goals? What did it feel like? Why did it matter to them so much?

So it's not surprising that one day I would write biographies.

When I start writing a new book, I spend months researching. I try to find primary sources like letters, diaries, and eyewitness accounts. It's a great way to get to know the person I'm writing about. In primary sources, I can find intimate details that bring them to life.

Take John Adams, for example. I knew a lot about him when I started writing my book *Those Rebels, John & Tom*. I knew he joined the Continental Congress in Philadelphia. And I knew he worked hard to convince the other delegates to vote for independence.

But I didn't know much about him as a person. So I read his diary. It turns out, he was very excited about the *food* he ate in Philadelphia. He especially loved desserts.

"A most sinful feast again! Everything which could delight the eye or allure the taste. Curds and creams, jellies, sweetmeats of various sorts, 20 sorts of tarts, fools, trifles, floating islands and whipped syllabubs."

Primary sources showed me that the champion of democracy had a real sweet tooth. (And in case you are curious, a whipped syllabub is a frothy mixture of sweetened whipped cream, lemon juice, and wine.)

Another wonderful source of information is letters. I knew that the philosopher Ralph Waldo Emerson loved living in Concord, Massachusetts. I knew he valued the idea of community. But it was reading this letter that showed me what a warm and welcoming friend he must have been.

> *Dear Mr. Thayer, July 3, 1872*
> *Come be a brave good cousin and face our heats*
> *and solitudes on Friday eve . . . and we will give you a*
> *cup of tea and piece of a moon and all the*
> *possibilities of Saturday . . .*

Sometimes, I write about people who were themselves writers. First Lady Eleanor Roosevelt began a newspaper column in 1935 and kept on writing it for almost thirty years. And when I read in one of her columns that she liked hot dogs, it brought her instantly to life.

It's through reading primary sources that I can spend time with people I admire. I can discover through their own words who they were and how they felt. It gives me insight into their values and character. And it allows me—in the best of all possible ways—to be a snoop.

44. Reading provides a lifeline when everything is different

by Sabina Khan

When I looked around the schoolyard, I saw my new classmates clustered in small groups, laughing and talking, comfortable with one another and their surroundings despite the sweltering November afternoon. Having recently moved from Germany to Bangladesh, I was displaced, plucked from everything familiar to me—the sounds, the people, the food, and even the air. Especially the air. Every breath I took alienated me. I was alone in one of the most densely populated countries in the world. My country. My people. But it didn't feel like that yet. And it wouldn't for a long time.

Every day after lunch we had library period and I would walk around the dimly lit room, wandering along the few shelves that lined the walls. I didn't understand any of the words because I hadn't learned how to speak in English yet. Or Bengali. I always had the strange sensation of being underwater and not being able to make sense of what people above the surface were saying. I could tell by the expressions on their faces if they were losing patience with me or found me so foreign that they couldn't relate to me at all, despite the fact that on the outside I was just like them, a brown-skinned eight-year-old girl. I wanted nothing more than to go back to my real life in Germany, but I knew that wasn't possible.

One day the librarian noticed me standing in front of a row of books. He came to me and asked me what kind of books I liked to read. When I couldn't answer him, he walked me over to a different bookshelf and pulled out a book. It had stories about pioneer children in the Wild West. I took it home and read it cover to cover with my mother watching over me and an English-German dictionary by my side. After I finished it, I went back for more and didn't stop until I had read the entire shelf. I read stories about hardship and new surroundings, about bravery and spirit, and even though these stories were about children I had nothing whatsoever in common with, they still resonated with me.

Books became my lifeline to this new world I found myself in, where everyone already knew everyone else and I was the only newcomer. In stories I could lose myself and forget the hurt and resentment that reminded me every minute of the day that I was an outsider. I devoured Enid Blyton's boarding school series because it was a connection to my old life, where I used to read these same stories in German. I read her mystery series because the characters were so familiar even in a different language.

One day during lunch, instead of going outside, I decided to stay in the classroom and read. I didn't notice when my classmates came back in, and when I looked up, I saw one of them smiling at me. She was holding up a book in the series I was reading. That was the first of many things we shared over the years, and that was the first time I knew I would be all right.

Books have always been a lifeline for me since then. Even as a young immigrant, at twenty-six years old, I found myself turning to books for solace and to find my place in this new life I had embarked on. This time I devoured stories of immigrants who, like me, had traveled halfway across the world to build a new life. These stories connected me to something much bigger than myself and allowed me to see myself as part of a larger picture. But most of all, at each stage in my life when I've felt invisible, books have made me feel seen and have given me a voice. It's the voice I've used to rebuild my life countless times, to teach my children to stand on their own feet, proud of and strong in their identities. And it's the voice I use when I write my stories, hoping that they will inspire others and give them strength, the way stories have always done for me.

READING CONNECTS US TO THE WORLD

WORDS AND PICTURES BY
KAZU KIBUISHI

MY BROTHER (TAKA) AND I WERE BORN IN TOKYO, JAPAN, AND MOVED TO CALIFORNIA IN 1981. I WAS THREE YEARS OLD AND TAKA WAS TWO.

WE HAD BARELY BEGUN SPEAKING JAPANESE WHEN ALL OF A SUDDEN WE HAD TO LEARN A NEW LANGUAGE IN A NEW COUNTRY.

MY GRANDMA AND MOM OPENED A RESTAURANT IN GARDENA AND IT WAS THERE THAT I DEVELOPED A LOVE FOR READING, AND IT BEGAN WITH READING COMICS.

I READ *MAD* MAGAZINE, MANGA, SUPERHEROES, AND COMIC STRIPS. ANYTHING WITH DRAWINGS THAT COULD HELP ME UNDERSTAND WORDS THAT WERE STILL NEW TO ME.

I ESPECIALLY LOVED FINDING COMICS AND CARTOONS AT THE SCHOLASTIC BOOK FAIRS.

AFTER SCHOOL, TAKA AND I WOULD HELP OUT AT THE RESTAURANT TO PASS THE TIME.

WE PEELED VEGETABLES AND RECEIVED COINS FOR THE ARCADE MACHINES AS A REWARD.

WHILE TAKA SHOWED A STRONG TALENT FOR PLAYING GAMES, MATH, AND STRATEGY, I CONTINUED TO DRAW CARTOONS.

TAKA GREW UP TO BECOME A VERY RESPECTED AND HIGHLY SUCCESSFUL AEROSPACE ENGINEER. HE'S ONE OF MY BIGGEST HEROES.

ONE CHRISTMAS, MY GODPARENTS, JUNI AND YAE SUGINO, GAVE ME A BOOK THAT WOULD CHANGE MY LIFE.

THE BOOK WAS TITLED *HOW-TO-DRAW: TIPS FROM THE TOP CARTOONISTS* AND IT FEATURED DRAWING ADVICE FROM SOME OF MY FAVORITE CARTOONISTS, LIKE *MAD MAGAZINE* ARTIST MORT DRUCKER. I STUDIED THIS BOOK MORE THAN ANY OTHER I HAVE READ.

IN HIGH SCHOOL, I FELL IN LOVE WITH CLASSIC LITERATURE.

I READ BOOKS BY JOHN STEINBECK AND ERNEST HEMINGWAY, AND WATCHED A LOT OF CLASSIC CINEMA, TOO.

THEY HELPED INSPIRE ME TO DEVELOP MY SKILLS AS A WRITER.

I WAS DETERMINED TO MAKE A COMIC THAT COULD HAVE THE SAME IMPACT AS MY FAVORITE WORKS OF CLASSIC LITERATURE AND CINEMA.

DURING MY SECOND YEAR OF COLLEGE, I BEGAN TO WORK ON *AMULET* FOR THE VERY FIRST TIME.

OVER TWENTY YEARS LATER, I AM STILL ON THIS JOURNEY, STILL WORKING TO CREATE VISUAL LITERATURE AND HOPEFULLY INSPIRING PEOPLE TO READ ALONG THE WAY!

46. Reading helps people feel

by Amy Sarig King

I love reading because it helps me find my feelings. It helps me escape them, too. It's the same reason I love writing. And looking at the night sky, and taking walks in nature, and canoeing. For me, it's pretty much all the same—whatever I'm doing connects to how I'm feeling.

When I was a little kid, I was aware of my emotions. Not in control of them, mind you, but aware of them. I was also very aware that certain emotions were not allowed at certain times, by certain people. This posed a problem for me because I believed then, at age four, as I believe now, at age fifty, that emotions are very important personal things and that no one else can tell a person how to feel or when to feel.

But in between, reader—in between ages four and forty-nine—I started to pretend that I didn't have feelings. I did it to stay safe from people who got angry at my emotions. I did it to hide my real feelings from people who would be cruel if they knew I was not feeling the way they wanted me to feel. I did it because I had to be tough, and as a woman, tough meant not showing my feelings. *Especially* any feelings that anyone could label "negative."

Oh, reader.

What a world we live in when we are taught to believe that we should be happy all the time. What a lie we are being asked to live.

And live that lie, I did. For many years. On the outside, I looked as happy as everyone wanted me to look. On the inside, I still had all kinds of feelings, and I wrote them down in my journals and in poems, and I read books that made me feel seen. I read *Where the Wild Things Are* because it made me feel like it was okay to be mad. I read all of Paul Zindel's novels as a teenager because he made me feel like I was going to be okay as long as I was honest and true to myself.

Now that I publish books, I get to write novels that encourage readers to feel things. I get letters that say, "I cried for hours after this book," and while me liking that sounds like I want people to cry, well, that would be accurate. I *do* want people to cry, because sometimes life hands you things that make you cry. And I want young people to feel angry because life hands us all kinds of things to be angry about, and I want young people to feel like they are allowed to feel and allowed to think about those feelings and allowed to talk about those feelings. Our world so often tells us to shut up about our feelings and I think it's hurting us as people. I *know* it's hurting us as people.

I love reading because it helps people feel. There are scientific studies that prove that reading improves empathy, quality of life, and especially your connection with your own emotions. I have finally learned that feelings are great things to have. I want you to think that, too. Hiding yourself from the world is no way to live. And once we realize that every emotion we have is important, the more real happiness we will have in our lives. It's a win-win! Trust me. Feel stuff. Read books. Write poems. Be proud. Be you. Feelings and all.

47. Reading lets you know you're not the only one

by Bill Konigsberg

When I was young, I thought I was the only gay kid in the world.

This was the 1980s. Before the Internet. It was also before there were a significant number of characters who were LGBTQIA+ on television or in books.

I loved books, and I devoured them. I read all my sister's Judy Blume books, and I adored them, but still I didn't really see myself in them. I didn't see any kids who were keeping my secret from their family, the one that made me feel different and alone.

And that made me feel very alone.

That all changed one day when I found a bookstore in New York City, where I lived, called the Oscar Wilde Bookshop. It was a bookstore devoted to LGBTQIA+ readers. I'd never known such a place existed, but here it was, a store with walls of books with people who were like me in this one important way.

I was seventeen when I found that store, and I bought a lot of books. I read one called *Tales of the City*, which was about a group of people in San Francisco who all felt like misfits, like me. They were also all kind. Some were gay, some were straight, some were bi, some were trans. It was the first time I saw people who shared my heart, who had struggled with feeling alone and sometimes felt sad, but also sometimes didn't, and who wanted to make the world a better place but sometimes messed up.

That book changed me forever. I've felt alone since, like all people do sometimes, but I've never felt quite as alone as I did before.

And now I get to be on the other side. I write books about LGBTQIA+ youth, and I get to meet some of those young people, and it makes me feel so happy when I see that same look in their eyes. That they are finally able to read books where they see parts of themselves for maybe the first time.

And it's books, more than anything else. More than TV or movies. Because reading a book is a far more personal experience than watching a show or movie. It's more interactive. It puts us in the middle of a situation, or acquaints us with a character in a more personal way. That's why I love books so much: for their ability to touch my heart.

To be able to write these sorts of books, like the ones that helped me? It is literally the best feeling I've ever had. To know I'm giving back the gift I got.

48. Reading gets you through the storm

by Gordon Korman

I'm crouched under a heavy library table with four Texas teachers and we could all be dead in the blink of an eye.

According to the schedule, I should be in the cafeteria, presenting to an audience of three hundred kids. But the National Weather Service spotted a line of tornadoes, due west and heading our way. The three hundred kids are sitting up against the library walls right now—and walls throughout the school—in the duck-and-cover position.

You might remember these tornadoes. If you've ever seen the YouTube clips of eighteen-ton semis being tossed violently around a parking lot by a powerful twister, *that's* what's bearing down on us. Of course, we don't know that at the time. All we have is weather radar of the storm system on one of the teacher's phones. And we're directly in its path.

To be honest, the teachers seem pretty calm about this, and so do the students. This is Dallas, where tornado alerts in April are kind of business as usual. The only person freaking out is the Canadian-born, New York–based visiting author. I've never lived anywhere twisters are a problem. The sum of my tornado knowledge is that they're capable of a) carrying Dorothy and Toto over the rainbow, and b) a lot of other things, all of them scary. I don't want to look like a baby in front of the kids, but I'm literally shaking.

So I peer out from under the table at the books on the nearby stacks. A faded spine catches my eye—*Tales of a Fourth Grade Nothing* by Judy Blume. Rising above my terror, I reach out and pluck the weathered paperback from the shelf. I can't help myself. When I was a kid, *Tales of a Fourth Grade Nothing* was *my* book. I was in fourth grade when it was new. It was the first time I really saw myself in a novel. In a way, it's responsible for my entire career. My first book was a school project. I could have written anything. But thanks to Judy Blume and Beverly

Cleary, *The Great Brain* and *The Mad Scientists' Club*, it was natural for my storytelling to take the form of a classic old-fashioned middle grade novel. I'm the writer I am because of the reader I used to be.

I'm transported into the world of Peter Hatcher and his brother, Fudge, and instantly I'm nine years old again, and no longer crouched under a table waiting for a twister to blow the school away. The next thing I know, a bell is ringing. Wonder of wonders, it isn't the kiss-your-butt-goodbye alarm. It's the all clear!

The kids are already filing out of the library. The teachers have all crawled out from under my table. I'm the only one still huddled there, lost in my reading.

"Where's everybody going?" I ask.

"To the cafeteria," the librarian replies. "For the author assembly."

Oh, right. That would be me.

Props to those Texas kids. They're a fantastic audience ten minutes after a life-and-death near miss. As for their visiting author, he makes it through too—with a little help from Peter and Fudge.

I can't say that's my number one reason to love reading, or even number one hundred. But it's very high on the list when I look back on that day.

49. Reading gets you excited to create

by Jarrett J. Krosoczka

50. Reading introduces you to inspiring people

by Kirby Larson

Her name was Mitsue Shiraishi. And we met in the best way possible: through the written word.

Later I would come to know the book of Mitsi: a good student who played high school basketball. After graduation, she cared for her elderly parents. Tended the family strawberry farm. Doted on a terrier mix named Chubby.

At our first encounter, she was a mere paragraph in a book titled *Strawberry Days: How Internment Destroyed a Japanese American Community*. I didn't even know if Mitsi was a child or an adult. But those first few words were sufficient to give me a sense of her heart. Her determination. Her courage.

In 1942, Franklin Roosevelt signed Executive Order 9066, which spoke to creating areas from which "any and all persons may be excluded." But the intent of the order wasn't to exclude any and all. And there was no "may" about it. The intent was to "exclude" every single person who looked like the enemy. In the end, FDR's autograph forced about 120,000 people of Japanese descent (most of them American citizens) from their homes and into incarceration camps. Mitsi was among them.

With no idea where she'd end up, she packed what she could into the two suitcases allowed. Would she need warm-weather clothes? Sweaters and galoshes? Somehow such decisions were made. Maybe, like others, Mitsi sold her sewing machine. A piano. The family car. All for pennies on the dollar to those who fed on the misery of the soon-to-be incarcerated. It was March when it was Mitsi's time to go. Strawberries were left to bloom, ripen, and rot in her family's carefully tended fields.

Thousands of people were forcibly removed from their homes. Thousands ended up in desolate places with ironic names: Camp

Harmony. Heart Mountain. Thousands lined up for dreary meals of Vienna sausage and boiled potatoes. Waited their turns to use glorified outhouses.

If thousands shared Mitsi's story, why did reading those few lines about *her* affect me so deeply?

Blame it on one word: Chubby.

It turns out, Mitsi was as besotted with Chubby as I was with my dog, Winston. My love for Winston led me to share a bed with four paws and a wiggly tail, cook special foods, buy dog toys by the dozen.

Mitsi's love for Chubby led her to take on the US Army.

In those sentences where we first met, I learned that Mitsi tried to follow all the rules for evacuation. But rule number three stated: "No pets of any kind shall be permitted." Mitsi was leaving her neighbors, her home, her farm; surely her country wouldn't separate her from Chubby. She wrote the general in charge, begging to be allowed to take her beloved four-legged friend.

That request was denied.

Neither Mitsi's letter nor the general's has survived. But those were words I did not need to examine. Mitsi's action spurred me to actions of my own, including reading everything I could about the incarceration; wonderful research librarians helped me uncover the meticulously kept diary of the superintendent of education at Minidoka, one of the ten incarceration camps. My reading led me to Judy Kusakabe, Mitsi's stepdaughter, who welcomed this complete stranger into her family's story, sharing rare and precious ephemera—camp yearbooks, diaries, photos.

Meeting Mitsi on the page inspired me to write a novel, *Dash*, featuring a young girl separated from her beloved dog. Even more rewarding, those few lines have inspired kid—and adult—readers all over this country to delve deeper into a shameful slice of American history. It all happened because of something I read. All because of one person.

Her name was Mitsue Shiraishi.

51. Reading makes you who you are

by Kathryn Lasky

There is a country in my head that would not be there if I didn't read. I read because I am. I am because I read. The Kathryn Lasky that exists now is because of reading. But I was co-parented by two wonderful people—Hortense and Marven Lasky—and by books, thousands upon thousands of books. The words I have read run like a stream through my mind. Where would I be without Scout Finch, Mary Lennox, Holden Caulfield, Scarlett O'Hara, Dorothy and (oh dear) the Tin Woodman? For as the Tin Woodman in *The Wizard of Oz* said to the Scarecrow, who desperately wanted brains: He would rather take a heart, "for brains do not make one happy, and happiness is the best thing in the world."

I am happy—but, yes, sometimes sad—because I read. But without stories I would be incomplete. My world would be colorless. My capacity for empathy stillborn. Books helped make me. And now I make books. I have come full circle in this universe of words.

52. Reading makes us all detectives

by Peter Lerangis

I was lying on my bed, shivering uncontrollably. On a humid, ninety-degree summer night in a room with no air-conditioning, this was not normal. I didn't scream for my parents because my teeth chattered. With shaky hands, I put down the book I was reading. And I did what any perfectly healthy eleven-year-old would do.

I freaked.

Swinging my legs around, I took deep breaths. Maybe I had the flu. Or some rare toxic crud carried to Long Island on the winds of the Gulf Stream. Or growing pains. Whatever those were.

My uncle and aunt were visiting, so I felt weird about walking downstairs in my shivery state and pleading for h-h-h-help.

Besides, I was dying to get back to my short story. It was called "To Build a Fire," by one of my favorite adventure writers, Jack London. Earlier that year I'd read his awesome novel *Call of the Wild*, and that evening I'd cracked open a collection of his stories.

Skin tingling, I bravely flung myself back onto the bed. The book was splayed open, facedown. The cover showed a dog or wolf racing across a bleak, snowy landscape. Here's what I remember about the story: a man and his husky are stranded in a blizzard. They run out of food far from civilization, with no way of navigating. As the dog begins to falter, the man struggles to feed it and keep it alive—even though he knows this might risk his own life. Sure enough, he soon grows weak. He's just about dead when the dog begins to protect him. It's a story about survival, about the love and devotion between animals and humans. But all you're thinking as you read it is *one of them is going to die.*

I picked it up and resumed reading. My shivering started again, but I ignored it. After I finished, all I could do was lie there, stunned. Letting the story bang around inside my brain. Thinking, thinking, thinking. And that's when I realized what was wrong with my body.

It was the book.

It was Jack London's fault.

It was words. Just *words*.

Somehow these little squiggles of ink had reached inside me like a virus. Only this didn't cause sickness. This felt more awesome than anything I'd ever experienced.

I had to share it with someone.

My dad would get it. I knew that. He was in the den, so I ran downstairs, grabbed the knob, and flung open the door. "Dad! Dad, I just—"

I saw him on the sofa next to my uncle, both of them intently watching a baseball game on TV. It must have been a great game, because they were screaming at the screen.

My dad turned to me and said hi, what's up. Or maybe he didn't. All I remember is that the feeling was starting to fade. The freezing cold. The excitement. The strangeness of what had just happened to me. It was leaking out, like the air from a balloon.

I knew it wasn't the right moment.

If I said anything, that feeling would lose power. Maybe forever. It felt that fragile. And I was *not* ready to let it go. So without saying another word, I quietly pulled the door shut and said nothing.

Thumping back upstairs into my room, I began reading the story again. But now I wasn't reading for the action or the plot. I was reading like a detective. I wanted to find Jack London's secrets.

How did he do it? I mean, every writer used the same ingredients— nouns, verbs, adjectives, etc. But as I read, I saw that the trick was in other things. Rhythms. Withheld information. Rich word choices. Creative absences of information. I wasn't sure about any of this, but it was thrilling to see even a bit behind that kind of power.

As I put the book down, I imagined being able to do something like that myself—to make other people *feel*, actually feel in the gut, using nothing but words. Up till then I'd never imagined anything I could do for a living. But this? If I could even come close to doing this, there could be no better way to spend a life.

I still feel that way. I feel lucky to wake up each morning to give it another try—and grateful for that long-ago evening, when chills caused me to become a writer.

I owe it all to Jack.

53. Reading is for curious cats

by Sarah Darer Littman

Do you ask a lot of questions? Do the grown-ups in your life ever get tired of you asking, "Why?"

If so, we've got a lot in common, because that was me as a kid. In fact, it's still me as an adult.

You've probably heard the old proverb *curiosity killed the cat* as warning against asking too many questions. But if that were true, I would be six feet under. Pushing up daisies. Deceased.

Writers tend to be very curious people.

It turns out that proverb couldn't be more wrong. Curiosity is what drives us to learn and discover. According to a study by the Pew Research Center, some of the key skills needed to succeed in today's jobs—and especially the future jobs that will be available when you grow up and enter the workforce—are "emotional intelligence, curiosity, creativity, adaptability, resilience, and critical thinking."*

What's really interesting is that these are skills even the most sophisticated artificial intelligence can't replicate. They're the skills that make us most human.

Can you imagine one of the best ways to learn these skills? You guessed it—reading books!

But don't just take that from me. In a 2015 interview, former US president Barack Obama said: "The most important stuff I've learned I think I've learned from novels. It has to do with empathy. It has to do with being comfortable with the notion that the world is complicated and full of grays, but there's still truth there to be found, and that you have to strive

---

* Rainie, Lee. "Skills Required for Future Jobs: 10 Facts." *Pew Research Center: Internet, Science & Tech*, Pew Research Center, 19 June 2018, https://www.pewresearch.org /internet/2018/06/19/skill-requirements-for-future-jobs-10-facts/.

for that and work for that. And the notion that it's possible to connect with some[one] else even though they're very different from you." *

I'm with President Obama. By reading books, I've been able to travel the world while still snuggled under the covers. I've imagined myself as a wizard, a queen, and a knight; as a scientist and an explorer; as a detective and a journalist, as a spy and a soldier. Perhaps most importantly, reading helps me to understand and connect with people who might lead lives that are very different from mine. It's helped me recognize that even if we come from different cultures, speak a different language, or practice a different religion, we share common emotions, hopes, and dreams.

As a writer, I've always been the most curious about exploring what happens in those complicated gray areas President Obama mentioned. Why do people make the decisions they do when the answers aren't clear-cut? Would I make the same decision or a different one if I found myself in the same circumstances? Books give us curious cats a chance not just to explore other lives, but also to think about and discuss ethics, a subject that doesn't seem to get nearly enough attention.

So ignore the naysayers and give your curiosity license to explore. Read more books—you'll be amazed at all the things you can discover!

---

* Robinson, Marilynne, and Barack Obama. "President Obama & Marilynne Robinson: A Conversation-II." *The New York Review of Books*, 19 Nov. 2015, https://www.nybooks.com/articles/2015/11/19/president-obama-marilynne-robinson-conversation-2/.

54. Reading gives us courage

by Natalie Lloyd

Reading opened my heart to worlds that had no limits.

This was a big deal for me. Because my real world felt crowded with them. (Limits, I mean.)

There are the usual, standard limits I don't think much about, like gravity and traffic rules. But there are others, too, physical ones, that I still work through daily. I was born with a brittle bone disease called osteogenesis imperfecta. This meant spending elementary and middle school in a wheelchair, or using a walker, because my bones weren't strong enough to handle a fall. Or an accidental bumping-into. I had lots of clunky casts, surgeries, physical therapy, and endless reminders to be careful. I often overheard people say that I was fragile.

When I read a book, however, I never felt fragile.

Or broken.

Or like I had to be careful.

I didn't feel limited at all.

Reading has been a snicker of magic for me, always.

The first time I felt book magic was when I read the Narnia series in elementary school. It was as if the air in the room changed when I opened the cover and read the first line, like some cheesy scene in a movie. My skin prickled on account of the (fictional) Narnia snow. The (fictional) lamppost in the forest was so vivid in my imagination that it felt like a real memory, not just a scene in a book. Lucy's wild courage got tangled up inside me somehow. And Aslan's roar became a permanent part of my heart. (When I ended up in the hospital for a broken leg, I would sometimes close my eyes through painful procedures and imagine I was holding on to Aslan.)

Those stories were fictional. I get that. But the courage that I found in the pages—in zillions of pages from other stories I loved—was real.

Books became a constant, gentle reminder that I wasn't alone in my feelings or fears. My favorite fictional friends like Anne Shirley, Kristy Thomas, Fern Arable, pretty much every character Judy Blume ever wrote, and (later on) Luna Lovegood all had scary, difficult, or impossible-feeling circumstances in their world. They battled bullies and dark wizards and phantom phone callers. I think we all have battles happening, too.

Not with dark wizards or phantom phone callers, hopefully.

But I think maybe we're all a little bit fragile in places, whether it's brittle bones or broken hearts or tough memories that still make us cry. Like our favorite characters, we're stronger than we know. We all have stories to tell. And we're all wildly unlimited in our hearts, imaginations, and ability to add a little kindness and hope to the world.

We're all kings or queens in Narnia, whenever we want to be. Or need to be.

Sometimes courage is just a page turn away.

55. Reading makes you feel seen (without having to explain yourself)

by Tracy Mack

The woods behind our house were my sanctuary. Every weekend, book in hand, I'd slip away from the breakfast table, sidle past the rust-battered swing set, and brave the prickly vines and creeping poison ivy to my spot. Harriet came with me. And Margaret and Deenie and Ramona and Fudge and Sally. Here in my own tiny forest, I was liberated from my oldest brother's inescapable rock music, his angry drums that shook the house, and the stream of unsavory, mop-haired boys who rehearsed in our basement.

I'd stretch out on a flat rock and settle in for a trip to Manhattan or suburban New Jersey or Portland, Oregon. Sometimes I'd climb the biggest oak and curl into the hammock of its wide, low branch. Something about nature's furniture and the loamy smell of damp earth and sun-kissed leaves set my imagination free and allowed me to sink deeply into another world. Even now, I love reading outside best of all. It's there that I feel most connected to something larger than myself.

Because I'd read the same books—*Harriet the Spy*; *Are You There, God? It's Me, Margaret.*; *Deenie*; all the Ramona books and the Fudge books; and my favorite, *Starring Sally J. Freedman as Herself*—so many times, we connected and reconnected like old friends. As they invited me into their inner worlds, I felt safe to commune things I only dimly understood about my eldest brother's volatile behavior. My book friends kept my secrets and provided pleasant distractions. I felt seen without having to explain myself.

On the best weekend mornings, my day would start long before breakfast, when my middle brother and I dragged from his closet a massive clear garbage bag filled with *Archie* comics. I relished the dramas between Betty and Veronica—and especially this time with my brother, reading side by side on our bellies, quiet together in a contented, storied silence.

Before bed, my mother read to me, often the same books I'd already read on my own. She was a bookworm and had once aspired to be an actress, so she was skilled with expression. All these years later, I can still hear her interpretation of Judy Blume's Fudge. Curled up in bed just the two of us, with my mother's melodic, Boston-laced voice washing over me and Fudge's misadventures amusing me, I was at ease and transported. And so was she, temporarily relieved of her preoccupation with my brother, and sharing her favorite entertainment with me.

Even though my early years were filled with books, I didn't consider myself a *reader*. I wasn't in the highest reading group at school; I didn't have wide-ranging taste; and I had no interest in newspapers or adult novels like my best friend did. I deemed myself mediocre. It wasn't until high school and college that I began to explore more deeply. And it wasn't until much later that I understood that the very act of reading—be it comic books or the same books time and again—made me a reader.

I'm glad I didn't count myself out. If I had, I would have missed so much connection and comfort, joy and discovery. And I might not have become a writer. Reading opened the world to me and showed me that as humans, we may be flawed, fearful, and fragile, but we are whole, and we are all longing for the same things: visibility, empathy, community, and above all, love.

56. Reading makes you less alone

by Carolyn Mackler

I was a "weird" kid. I was "cute" enough and "friendly" enough that most people assumed I was "normal." But I wore a thatched flowerpot on my head (around the neighborhood, third grade). I wrote illustrated picture books about meeting Hitler (fourth grade). I wore plaid dresses because I liked to pretend I went to a fictional boarding school (fifth grade; the other girls wore designer jeans). The last bit about the boarding school dresses probably contributed to why things tanked socially in middle school. Boys snickered at me and girls edged away from being my friend and teachers did nothing to help. I began to feel lost and alone. And while I always loved reading, middle school is when novels saved my life.

In books I found characters who were quirky like me or felt alone like I did. I found characters who didn't fit in—or sometimes I found characters who were having a blast because it wasn't all bad. Often I was having plenty of fun and I wanted to read about adventurous kids who were enjoying their childhoods as much as I was. I had a best friend, a loyal dog, and loving parents. That helps when your school life stinks.

I love reading because it has always made me feel more connected, less alone. And that is exactly why I write. In my most recent novel, *Not If I Can Help It*, I wrote about eleven-year-old Willa. She has sensory processing disorder. That means her brain processes stimuli differently than most people. Socks with itchy seams make Willa want to scream and mushy foods make her want to gag and sometimes she shrieks and hops around and wants to be squished. My son, who is now a teenager, struggled with sensory processing disorder when he was younger. I did too when I was a kid. As my son was dealing with his disability, there were times when he felt judged by other kids—and I felt judged by other parents. That's why I wrote Willa's story. I wanted to write a book that someone like my son, or a kid like me, would have loved to read. The best thing is that since *Not If I Can Help It* has come out, I've gotten letters from readers telling me that they have sensory processing disorder or they hate itchy seams. They thank me for writing Willa's story and helping them feel less alone!

Hey, did you notice that I put "weird" and "cute" and "friendly" and "normal" in quotes? Now that I'm a grown-up, I've realized something huge. MAJOR. Those words mean zilch. When I was a kid I thought that weird = bad. I thought that cute = the blond girl who smiled a lot. I thought that normal = the family who was definitely not mine. I thought that friendly = the chatty person who always knew the right thing to say. But it's NOT true, okay? So obliterate those words from your vocabulary and be yourself. In fact, read this again and substitute those four words in quotes for "awesome" or "happy." Ahhhh, much better!

57. Reading can satisfy our curiosity . . . or fire it up

by Ann M. Martin

Reading (and books, stories, and storytelling) has been part of my life for as long as I can remember. My parents read to my sister and me before we knew how to talk. In the evenings, when Jane and I were older, we would curl up on the couch with our parents while one or the other read to us from *The Wizard of Oz* or *Charlotte's Web* or the books by Beatrix Potter. My father made up stories about a tiny man named Mr. Piebald who lived in the apartment-building oak tree in the woods behind our house. He told us Mr. Piebald stories for years.

When I was young I read every day, but I didn't stop to wonder *why* I loved reading. I just enjoyed it. Long after I was too old for picture books, I would wander into our den, scan the bookshelves, and pull out *Wait Till the Moon Is Full* by Margaret Wise Brown, or *The Little House* by Virginia Lee Burton, or *Millions of Cats* by Wanda Gág, all favorites. I would read them over and over, examining the pictures, then go back to my room and read *The Yearling* by Marjorie Kinnan Rawlings or *Rascal* by Sterling North—books for much older readers.

As an adult I still read every single day. I read while I eat meals, I read when I get in bed at night, I read on planes and trains and the subway, and I try to carve out a little chunk of time every morning, even just fifteen minutes, to settle myself. I like to go into a calm place in my head, clear out my thoughts, and focus on someone else's story.

So here's a secret: I'm also a bit nosy, which is another reason I like other people's stories. And when you get right down to it, it's one of the reasons I love reading. I want to know things, all sorts of things. What's in that box? Where did you grow up? How on earth are you going to get yourself out of the mess you've gotten into? As you can imagine, I particularly like mysteries. Who bonked the butler over the head? (The butler isn't always the culprit.) *Why* did someone bonk him? I like historical novels too. What did people eat three hundred years ago? What were their houses like? Biographies and memoirs are of particular interest because I get to find out details of the lives of real people. What could be better?

Of course, I also like words. Sometimes I'm in awe of the words a writer uses to describe something, whether that something is as ordinary as a shoe or as elusive as a feeling. I reread sentences that I particularly like, letting the words roll around in my head. I think about words. (Why is "Piebald" funny?) I like homophones; I even have favorite ones, "phrase" and "frays," "sword" and "soared."

Books and words tease our imaginations. They can satisfy our curiosity or they can fire it up. They make us think, they take us on journeys. And all from a few squiggles on paper.

58. Reading transports you

by Wendy Mass

I spent a lot of time staring at a poster that hung on the wall of my fourth-grade classroom—a drawing of a large ship parting the ocean. The quote on it was from poet Emily Dickinson: *There is no frigate like a book to take us lands away.* The large dictionary in the front of the class confirmed that a frigate was a fast, powerful boat.

At that point I hadn't had the experience of being transported anywhere by a book, and I really needed to be. My family was going through a rough patch. Home had suddenly become a confusing place and school was a welcome escape. One afternoon my teacher began reading to us from a big anthology made up of excerpts from different novels. The story she read that day was about four siblings who stepped into a wardrobe (which she explained was like a freestanding closet), and found themselves in a world called Narnia, full of magical talking creatures. I was captivated. My own problems fell away as I sat on the carpet, lost in this new world. I was too shy to ask the name of the book afterward (and I didn't want her to think I wasn't paying attention!). But as soon as it was our class's turn for our weekly trip to the school library, I began pulling books off the shelves, frantically searching for this story that had transported me in the way that the poster promised a book could do.

The librarian came to my rescue, gently asking me to describe what I was looking for. I told her as much as I remembered. A minute later she placed *The Lion, the Witch and the Wardrobe* by C. S. Lewis in my hands. I hungrily read the first page and knew this was the right one.

That book didn't leave my hands the whole week. I ate with it, I slept with it, I read it three times, cover to cover. During wartime, the four siblings found their escape in Narnia, where they were powerful and loved. Through their experiences, I, too, felt powerful and loved, and that feeling lasted even when I closed the book. When I reluctantly returned it the following week, the librarian reached below her desk and pulled out another book. "Here," she whispered, handing it to me like a secret. "I thought you might like this." I looked down at the cover, then hugged it to my chest. THERE WAS A SEQUEL! The librarian smiled and told me there were actually seven books in the Chronicles of Narnia series. I think I may have cried.

I have no doubt that reading about these ordinary kids having extraordinary adventures turned me into a reader, and years later, into a writer who wanted to make the next generation of readers feel the way that Narnia made me feel. A few years ago, I got a letter from a young reader that said, "Your book *11 Birthdays* is my favorite book. Even though I have a copy at home, I like to visit the copy on my school library's shelf, whenever it's checked in. Then today there was another book right next to it that I hadn't seen before. I pulled it out. It was called *Finally*, and the cover said it was a sequel to *11 Birthdays*. I screamed and hugged it. Thank you, thank you, thank you!"

Needless to say, getting this letter made me feel like my life had come full circle in the best possible way. So keep pulling books off the shelves until you find one that makes you not want to put it back. And then find more and more like that. As writer George R. R. Martin wrote, "A reader lives a thousand lives before he dies. The man who never reads lives only one." I wish you many, many lives.

59. Reading is like breathing

by Patricia C. McKissack

Long before I became a writer, I was a listener and an observer. My relatives, who were dynamic and skilled storytellers, helped develop my listening and observation skills before I could read or write.

On hot summer evenings our family would sit on the porch and listen to my grandmother tell a hair-raising ghost story, or my mother would recite Dunbar poems or Bible stories. Sometimes we'd get a real treat when my grandfather would dramatize an episode from his childhood, told in the rich and colorful dialect of the Deep South. I can still hear him beginning a yarn, saying: "It was back in nineteen and twenty-seven. I disremember the exact day, but it was long 'bout July, 'cause the skeeters was bitin' whole chunks outta my arms . . ."

When I was growing up, we kids called the half hour just before nightfall the dark-thirty. We had exactly half an hour to get home before the monsters came out.

During the hot, muggy summer, when days last longer, we gathered on the front porch to pass away the evening hours. Grandmama's hands were always busy, but while shelling peas or picking greens, she told a spine-chilling ghost tale about Laughing Lizzie, a specter who'd gone mad after losing her entire family in a fire. Her hysterical laughter was said to drive listeners insane.

Then on cold winter nights when the dark-thirty came early, our family sat in the living room and talked. The talk generally led to one of Grandmama's hair-raising tales. As the glimmers of light faded from the window overlooking the woods, she told about Gray Jim, the runaway slave who'd been killed while trying to escape. Gray Jim's ghost haunted the woods on moonless nights. "Sorry for those who hear Gray Jim's dying screams," she whispered, "'cause they're not long for this world."

At this point my grandmother would pause and say, "Pat, go in the kitchen and get me a glass of water."

Many years later I learned that Laughing Lizzie and Gray Jim had been real people in our small African American community. The strange—and often sad—circumstances of their deaths had inspired the ghost stories that lived after them. They inspired me, too.

As a youngster I had no idea that my heritage would one day be the springboard for my writing career.

Somewhere around age seven I discovered reading. And so began my lifelong love affair with the printed word, a passion I share with my husband and writing partner, Fred. To us, reading is like breathing; both are essential to life.

60. Reading brings you sharks, snakes, and . . . Ramona

by Kate Messner

Where I grew up, there were farms and apple orchards. Neighbors on our road knew whether you went straight up the hill to the house from the bus or not. It was a tiny village, with one store downtown where you could buy a dress for a school dance and one where you could buy new gym sneakers in September. There was no bookstore. But there was a friendly little library. And an elementary school that sent home Scholastic Book Club flyers each month.

I'd wait and wait for the day that flyer came home tucked in my folder. I'd go to my room, pull the cap off a fat Magic Marker, and sniff it (we had the ones that smelled of grape and orange) while I pored over the books on those flimsy newsprint pages. When I circled the ones I wanted, the marker bled through the page. Sometimes it was hard to tell if it was that shark book on page three that I wanted or the mystery on page four. That was okay because really I wanted them both. I wanted them *all*. Books were an escape from the be-careful rules and don't-go-far walls of my small town. They reflected my life back at me even as they taught me to imagine more.

The truth is, my favorite character of all was a girl a lot like me—Beverly Cleary's Ramona, who asked too many questions and made messes and got into lots of curiosity-fueled trouble. Remember the scene where Ramona made a crown of burrs (like the boy in the TV commercial . . . "Ta-da!") and got it hopelessly stuck in her hair? I read that over and over. Inspired by Ramona, I confiscated my father's cigarettes and replaced them with rolled-up paper warnings about the dangers of smoking. Like Ramona, I got in trouble. And like Ramona, I was forgiven. Her stories taught me it was okay to be curious, okay to be a little different.

My memories of Ramona are a big reason I've come to be such an advocate for books that feature characters from traditionally underrepresented backgrounds. As a white girl growing up in a small town, I got to see myself in stories all the time. Not everyone did, and knowing what that meant to me, growing up, makes me want it for all kids now.

The other books I circled over and over again in my flyers were nonfiction titles that were loaded with cool facts and photos. I'm not sure why—maybe it was the feeling that nothing happened in my small town?—but books about dangerous animals and natural disasters were my favorites. If there were wild tornadoes, sharks with razor-sharp teeth, or venomous snakes with glistening fangs on the cover, I circled that book as fast as I could. (Then I'd check to see what got accidentally circled on the next page when the marker bled through. An Encyclopedia Brown mystery? Perfect!)

I may have grown up in a small town, but my world never felt small, thanks to the books I read. It's no wonder that I became a writer, or that research is one of my favorite parts of the process, whether I'm exploring the historic beaches of Normandy or tracking giant tortoises in the Galápagos Islands. Reading planted the curiosity that fuels my life as an author today. The stories that landed on my desk each month taught me that there was a big world out there—a wild and fascinating place worth exploring and sharing every chance I'd get.

61. Reading gives you comfort

by Ellen Miles

Like all avid readers, I love reading for so many reasons. I read for excitement, adventure, and knowledge; for distraction, for connection, and, of course, for pleasure. But I also read for what I think is one of the best reasons to love reading: for comfort.

A friend of mine says she loves the books I write because all the stories have a guaranteed happy ending. "It says so, right on the front," she tells people. And so it does, there at the top of every one of the book covers: *The Puppy Place*—Where every puppy finds a home."

Kind of a spoiler, I guess—maybe it ruins the suspense for some readers, but it makes me happy to know that kids can dive into any one of my books without worrying too much about whether things will work out for the adorable foster puppy pictured on the cover. That kind of reading can be comforting, like a warm blanket you pull over yourself on a gray, drizzly day.

A happy ending isn't essential for comfort. Sometimes familiarity is comforting, like a book with characters and settings we know well. Sometimes neutral topics like bird identification or recipes for banana muffins will do the trick. Even murder mysteries can be comforting—there's a whole genre known as the "cozy," often set in a quiet British village.

Happy endings or not, I read for comfort when I am lonely or bored or sad, when I am sick or hurting, when I'm feeling the need for a treat and a banana muffin just won't cut it. I read cookbooks and comics; animal stories and tales of adventure; novels and nature guides; mysteries and series books (and some mystery series books, even though I'm really not a mystery reader). When I was fifteen and spent almost an entire summer in bed, sick with mononucleosis, I gobbled up books by P. G. Wodehouse (old-fashioned British comedy featuring Jeeves the butler) and Ian

Fleming (Bond, James Bond). When my mother died last year, I found respite from my grief in rereading books by Jane Austen, one of her all-time favorite authors. When I'm going through tough times, or just want to feel safe and secure, I love to revisit favorite books, the ones I've read over and over again, almost every year of my life since I was a child (*The Secret Garden*, *Harriet the Spy*, *Half Magic*, *A Wrinkle in Time*, *Beezus and Ramona*, *Understood Betsy*, Tintin comics, *The Jungle Book*).

The world can be a challenging place—more so all the time, it seems. We all need reliable friends, the kind who can be counted on to make us feel better. People may come and go from our lives, but books, and reading, will always be there. And that's a comfort.

62. Reading can be a shared experience

by Sarah Mlynowski

I fell in love with reading in the third grade. I devoured everything by Judy Blume, Gordon Korman, and every series I could get my hands on. Sweet Valley High! Fear Street! Nancy Drew! The Baby-sitters Club! What I loved about those books was that they made me feel connected. By book two, or even chapter two, I was meeting up and hanging out with old friends, like Fudge, or Bruno and Boots, or Nancy, or Mary Anne, Claudia, Stacey, and Kristy. No matter where I was—my bed, the back seat of my parents' car, my couch—if I had a book, I wasn't alone.

The thing about books, though, is that they don't just connect you to fictional characters. They help connect you to real people, too.

My friends Jess and Karen were also voracious readers. We discussed books we loved. We shared books we loved. We wanted to *live* in books we loved. After reading *The Friendship Pact* by Susan Beth Pfeffer, we wrote, performed, and recorded a forty-five-minute play based on the novel. After reading the Baby-sitters Club, we debated which characters we were most like. We decided I was a Kristy, Karen was a Stacey, and Jess was a Claudia. We even started a baby-sitters club of our own. We made flyers and hung them around town, and actually got baby-sitting jobs, although because we were only in sixth grade, our parents made us go in pairs. But still. It was like we were in the books. Together!

When you're reading a novel, you're sharing an experience. You are not the only one crying at the end of *Charlotte's Web*, or holding your breath during *Refugee*, or laughing through *Restart*. There are kids—and grown-ups—having the same feelings you are having about the same plot twist, the same description, the same joke. So even if you're reading on your own, you're never *truly* alone. These days when I read something amazing, I immediately text Jess and Karen: *OMG are you reading*

The Ballad of Songbirds and Snakes? *Let me know when you get to chapter five.*

I now have two daughters, Chloe, who is ten, and Anabelle, who is seven. My favorite activity in the world is lying on the couch beside them, all of us reading. My even more favorite activity is when we're all on the couch reading, and they're curled up with books *I've* read and loved. I try not to interrupt them every two minutes with questions: "What part are you on? Were you surprised? Isn't she the best?" But I can't always help myself.

Right now Chloe is reading her seventh Baby-sitters Club book. Anabelle is reading her first.

Chloe is definitely a Kristy like me, but Anabelle is such a Mary Anne.

63. Reading is a story in itself

by Jaclyn Moriarty

I grew up in Sydney, Australia, in a family of six children. We also had two dogs, two horses, a cat, a duck, and twelve chickens.

My mother did a lot of laundry. Clothes were always pegged to the line in our backyard. A note was always stuck to our fridge with a magnet:

If it rains, run for your life.

The note meant this: At the first sign of rain, you raced, like an Olympic sprinter, to the line, and rescued the laundry.

One day, there was a terrible storm in Sydney.

The day of this storm, my mother collected my youngest sister, Nicola, from high school. The sky was low with angry black clouds. Wind whipped leaves against the car. Thunder grumbled.

The car reached our driveway and stopped outside the garage. Nicola pressed the remote. The garage door opened.

And that's when the first raindrops hit.

"The laundry!" shrieked my mother.

She and Nicola leapt from the car and tore around to the backyard. They skidded to the clothesline. Their hands reached up—

I'll stop the story for a moment here, to tell you something.

Reading is strange. It's tangled up with the real world. There's no clear line saying: On this side is the story, and on that is true life. Instead, there's a fine, fine curtain between them, and it shivers and sways, looping back and forth between both.

In my home, we didn't have a TV, but we did have a playroom. There were daddy longlegs spiders in the corners, and a yellow bookcase against the wall. The bookcase was filled with my mother's collection of books from when she was a child. The bookcase was the focus of our days.

We didn't just read the books. We talked about them. We acted out scenes. Inspired by the characters in *What Katy Did*, we played Murder in the Dark. (Our parents banned the game because somebody always ended up smashing into something in the dark, and either breaking the object or their toe. But we played it anyway, in secret, which was even better.)

Any unexplained mystery in our house—who drew on the back of Dad's important documents? Why was there no milk when Mum knew she'd bought some?—turned us into detectives. We were Nancy Drew collecting clues. We formed clubs based on the rules of the Secret Seven club. After we'd read *James and the Giant Peach*, we ran outside and got trapped in a giant's jam sandwich. Most of the neighborhood kids were trapped along with us (and they still talk about that sticky situation). Sometimes our mother's books themselves became the game. We played Library, creating index cards for each book, and getting into screaming fights over who got to be the librarian.

Then we turned into teenagers and packed the books away.

And that brings me back to the story.

My mother and sister raced to the backyard. Skidded to the clothesline. Their hands reached up, and—

BOOM!!!!

They froze.

The air shook and vibrated around them. The dogs barked, the horses whinnied, the chickens squawked.

Mum and Nicola stared at each other.

And then they ran through the pouring rain back to the garage.

Only, the garage wasn't there.

In its place was a giant pile of rubble.

Lightning had struck the wall and smashed the garage to smithereens.

If they hadn't run for the laundry—if they'd driven into the garage—they'd have been stepping out of the car exactly when it happened.

Later that night, one of my sisters pointed out the note on the fridge:

If it rains, run for your life.

A chill ran through the room.

Later still, we remembered.

The books from the playroom had been packed in boxes in the garage.

Our childhood books—our mother's childhood books—were now crushed beneath a pile of muddy rubble.

It was sad, but also somehow right.

The books that had lit up our childhood were a story of their own. A story that had ended, as good stories should, with a thunderclap.

64. Reading, like a dog, can bring you great joy

by Robert Munsch

When I was four years old, I lived on a short, dead-end street called Green Avenue. Cars were a rarity on Green Avenue and the street was mostly a children's playground.

I don't remember adults saying, "Go play in the street," but that is what happened. So I went on explorations of the street. At the far end, there was a lady who had a Scotty dog. Not only did she have a Scotty dog, but she was so happy to have visitors, she always gave me milk and cookies after I played with Angus in the backyard.

We didn't have a dog. I became a sort of uncle to Angus.

One day my mother gave me a present. It wasn't a birthday present or a Christmas present. She explained it was a very special present, just for me. I unwrapped it, and it was a book called *Angus Lost*, by Marjorie Flack. The Scotty dog in the book looked exactly like my Angus.

My parents read many books to me, but this is the one I remember for the great joy it gave me when I was four.

Fifty years later, I decided I needed to replace the book. I tracked it down at a used bookstore in Australia. Bingo! I had the book.

Books let you go backward in time.

Reading Is an Act of Faith

by Jon J Muth

Every act of communication
is an act of faith.

The thought that I can make
marks here and now
and you will see them

and understand their meaning,
in the way that I intend

at some time in the future,
seems to me to be preposterous.

But that *is* what is happening.

Even if it is not perfect,
it is no less a miracle.

Reading is a belief in miracles.

I know we don't think of things that way very often.

Maybe because we are busy.

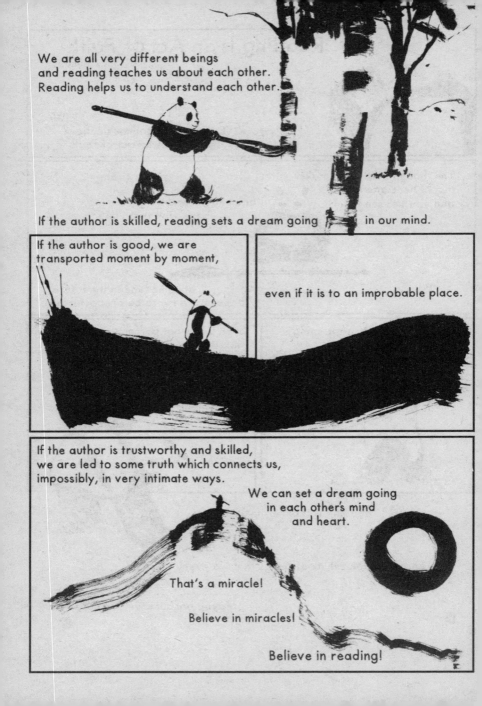

We are all very different beings
and reading teaches us about each other.
Reading helps us to understand each other.

If the author is skilled, reading sets a dream going in our mind.

If the author is good, we are transported moment by moment,

even if it is to an improbable place.

If the author is trustworthy and skilled, we are led to some truth which connects us, impossibly, in very intimate ways.

We can set a dream going in each other's mind and heart.

That's a miracle!

Believe in miracles!

Believe in reading!

66. Reading thrills with the wonder of language

by Walter Dean Myers

"Once I began to read, I began to exist."

Reading, for as long as I can remember, has always been a good part of my life. My reading habits as a young boy growing up in Harlem, New York, were similar to those of every avid reader. Did I read everything I could get my hands on? Of course I did. Did I read under the desk in school? Certainly. Did I have the flashlight under the covers to finish just one more chapter before falling asleep? Absolutely.

I can't imagine my life without the books I've enjoyed and the pleasures of reading. As a child I was thrilled with the wonder of language.

I believe that my reading "mind" was prepared long before I came to my first page of printed material. It began, and I am quite confident of this, in the conversations I had with my foster mom in our tidy Harlem apartment. My mother used to engage me in simple conversations as she did the housework each day. She didn't talk at me, she talked to me and expected me to answer her. I remember her asking me what the weather was like and how we should dress if we walked across 125th Street to the market stalls under the train trestle. I would dutifully go to the window, assess the weather, and decide what we should wear.

Sometimes she would ask me what I thought we might see on our crosstown journey, and I, pleased to have my opinion heard, would tell her. Would we take the crosstown trolley or walk? If I was asked I knew it meant that Mama had money for the trolley. It was quite all right with her if I made up something.

I remember Mama reading to me when I was five. Each day she would do the usual housework, which consisted of cleaning anything that needed cleaning, ironing anything that entertained the notion that it could possibly harbor a wrinkle, and putting away everything in its assigned place. Then, for that brief period between housework "done" and supper "started," she would read. Her choice of reading was always the same. True romance, love, heartbreak, jealousy, men as handsome as princes, and women whose bosoms rose and fell breathlessly from page to page. I didn't understand much about romance but I loved that time with Mama, sitting in our small kitchen, hearing her totally pleasant voice as she read. Did I tell you I was a mama's boy? I was.

What I knew about reading was that the print on the page was to be decoded and that Mama and I could do it. And when we did it we could enter the magical world of story. It allowed you to sit on your mother's lap and lean against her as you recreated the world in your own mind. Mama, who had only gone as far as the third grade in the small school in Pennsylvania she had attended, read with a finger moving slowly across the page.

I don't remember actually learning the decoding process. The vocabulary of those *True Love* and *True Romance* magazines must have been quite limited because I began recognizing printed words by the time I was five. By six, I could read to Mama as she worked, and she would correct the words I didn't know.

My father, Herbert Dean, did not read. That tragedy wouldn't catch up with me for decades. I was a mama's boy.

This selection was assembled from excerpts of Walter Dean Myers's 2009 Arbuthnot Lecture.

67. Reading is for rebels

by Jennifer A. Nielsen

In the 1970s, high fashion was the combination of brown, orange, and mustard. *Star Wars* made its debut. Also, I entered kindergarten.

Back then, few incoming students knew how to read. Kindergarten was the time to learn ABCs and maybe, if we worked really hard, we'd get around to basic words such as *stop* and *go*, which meant to me, "Stop learning and go take a nap."

But thanks to the teaching instincts of my older brother, I started that all-important year as a reader. I couldn't wait to dive into every book in the school.

There was only one problem:

I may have been assigned to the one teacher in the history of the universe who wasn't equally excited.

"You can learn to read in the first grade," she told me. "If you try to read now, you might do it wrong."

Wrong? Even at age five, that didn't make sense to me. Every *Sesame Street* episode I'd ever seen clearly stated that reading was wonderful. Even Oscar the Grouch said so.

Yet my teacher asked that I only look at the pictures of those books. But how could I stare at the words and pretend I didn't know what they said?

That very day, I made a decision to engage in the biggest rebellion of my life . . . well, up to age five.

I began sneak-reading. I mastered the art of pretending to look at pictures, while secretly I was reading every single word. *Stop* and *go* began to take on new meanings. Such as: "Never stop reading. Go get another book."

Maybe that's what my teacher meant by learning to read wrong.

Sneak-reading had a deep impact on me. It bonded me to books as perhaps nothing else could, because even in that small way, I had to fight for my right to read.

Little did I know then that others had fought for that same right, long before I ever did.

In 1842, teachers at the School for the Blind in Paris were ordered to burn their books written in Braille. They refused, risking their jobs and reputations, to protect the right of their students to read.

In 1948, the US government banned all comic books that refused to comply with their censorship guidelines, forcing many comic book writers into the underground. One young comic book writer defied the ban, eventually ending the regulations. His name was Stan Lee.

And in the 1800s, when the Russian Empire banned all Lithuanian-language books in that small country, the book smugglers rose up. These brave people left their country to get books printed in their own language. Then, at great personal risk, they smuggled them back inside their borders.

To do so was very dangerous. If they were caught—and many were—it often meant a one-way trip to Siberia, a prison of ice and snow. My book *Words on Fire* tells their story.

Writing the book began with this question: Why would people risk everything they had, even their own lives, for books?

I found my answer back in my kindergarten class, in the eyes of five-year-old me, sitting at a kindergarten table conducting the greatest rebellion of my life.

Defying my teacher for my right to read.

And in my own small and insignificant way, I suppose I became a book smuggler too.

68. Reading is a magic portal

by Garth Nix

When I was seven years old, I discovered the small library I had been visiting for years was more magical than I had ever known. I was in grade three at Turner Primary School in Canberra, Australia. For the first time I was allowed to walk to and from school. This was the late 1960s and Canberra was a very small city; there weren't many cars, and all the kids walked or rode their bikes.

Near the school there was a small street of shops, with a butcher, a newspaper shop, a sweet shop (where we'd buy two chocolate-covered caramels called cobbers for *one cent*), a general store, and . . . a children's library.

The library was small, not much more than a garden shed packed from floor to ceiling with books. I already loved it and had been visiting with my mother for years, once a week or so. I'd started there with picture books by John Burningham, Dr. Seuss, Maurice Sendak, Tomie dePaola, and many more, moving on to chapter books and even actual novels. I often couldn't really understand the bigger books but I wanted to read them anyway. Later on, I'd read a lot of these books again. Maybe this is where my lifelong habit of rereading favorite books began. I recommend this, because you can often get something different from a book when you read it again, particularly as you get older.

But I didn't really know what that library and the librarians in it could do until I did start walking home by myself in third grade and stopped off every day to return the book or books I'd read overnight and get new ones.

By this stage I'd read pretty much everything that tempted me on the shelves and I eagerly awaited the books that would appear on the "New Books" shelf.

Then, one day, I discovered that library didn't simply hold the books I could see on the shelves. I'd been reading an author who later would become a favorite. I can't remember exactly who it was. It might have been Susan Cooper, Diana Wynne Jones, Alan Garner, Lloyd Alexander, Andre Norton, Robert Heinlein, Rosemary Sutcliff, Joan Aiken, Elisabeth Beresford, Edward Eager, E. Nesbit . . . any one of these or many others.

Whoever it was, I asked the librarian if there were any more books by that writer. I meant in the library, even though I'd already looked myself.

She replied with a magic incantation.

"Not here, but we will get them in for you."

It was only then I understood. That tiny library, with perhaps two or three hundred books, was connected to the bigger libraries, and those libraries to other libraries, to a whole world of books. Thousands of books, hundreds of thousands of books. Maybe millions of books.

The library was a portal to other worlds. Worlds full of books, and those books contained other worlds in themselves as well. Every time I read one I was taken somewhere else, to real or imagined places different to my own, with amazing people doing incredible things. I could live other lives through books, and learn all kinds of things while simply enjoying a story.

That small children's library and all the books it brought to me have helped make me the person I am today. My reading life, as much as my actual life, has given me experiences that have guided my choices, have equipped me to understand and deal with opportunities and difficulties, from the smallest daily struggles to the big challenges. I read because I love to, but it has many benefits as well.

Reading also made me a writer. If you want to write, this is how it starts and continues, with reading. I hope you will be as lucky as I was, to have a magical library, a book-loving family, and access to all the books in the vast universe of wonderful reading.

69. Reading may be hard, but it's worth the trip

by Michael Northrop

For some people, reading comes easy. They're handed the right book as a kid, and away they go on a lifelong magic carpet ride of the imagination. Or something like that. Being an author, and often surrounded by very bookish people, I hear that story a lot. The metaphor varies (and is usually better), but the story remains the same.

Notably absent is any talk of the first step in that journey: the actual process of learning to read. The mental mechanics. When I think of what that process must have been like for these lifelong avid readers, I imagine that scene in *A Christmas Story*: "A plus plus plus plus!"

I have a different story. For me, that first step was a doozy. I am dyslexic. I repeated a grade and spent some time in special education. It was difficult and sometimes frustrating. I remember sitting at a small desk in the corner of a warm, sunny room and reading the same few *Dick and Jane*–type books over and over and over again. See Michael snore.

Most of all, it was isolating. After my second year in second grade, I was a year older than my classmates. For the rest of my childhood, I was terrified they would find out why. *Held back. Special ed.* I guarded these secrets fiercely. For years, I didn't even have birthday parties. I was too afraid of the words "How old are you now?"

Eventually, though, I began reading for fun. I was tricked into it by a game and some snappy costumes. The game was Dungeons & Dragons. I loved immersing myself in those imaginary adventures so much that it barely occurred to me that poring over and puzzling out the rulebooks even qualified as reading.

The snappy costumes belonged to superheroes. (My outfits, heavy on brown corduroys, were decidedly non-snappy.) Comic books were popular with my friends, available on a rack at the local pharmacy and—amazingly, miraculously—accessible to me. In fact, with their sparse, economical captions and emphasis on visual storytelling, I could read them nearly as fast as my classmates could. For the first time I was literally on the same page as my friends when it came to reading. The isolation began to crack.

Next came poetry. I liked it because it's short and you have to read it slowly and carefully—which was the only way I could read. Then came short stories. I was getting better at reading and enjoying it more. By high school, I was reading novels for fun, chugging through them slowly and diligently. I still sought out short books (I still do). If it had a front and back cover, it counted, and I loved that little victory of reaching the end of even the shortest book. Somehow, improbably, English had become my favorite subject.

And so, finally, bumpily, my little threadbare magic carpet arrived. I love it so. And I'm not alone. The more open I am about my early struggles with reading, the more people I hear from who shared them, in one form or another. From learning disabilities to second languages, there are many barriers. For some of us, reading is a joy not because it was always easy, but because it was difficult. It was a mountain that we had to climb, that we still climb, even if we find ourselves a few hundred yards behind the pack. Why do we climb that mountain? I guess we just like the view.

70. Reading takes you deeply into its world

by Daniel José Older

One of the first times I fell in love with reading, I was in Florida on a family vacation and bored out of my mind. The most exciting thing around was right in front of me, in the pages of *The Fellowship of the Ring*. There, some hobbits were trying to make a desperate escape from hooded riders on the outskirts of a small town on a rainy night. The riders had been trailing them for a while; they were terrifying and mysterious and I'd never read anything like it in my life, never felt so completely inside a book. What would happen next? What if the hobbits were caught? I had to keep reading.

The rain fell in sheets and the night was impossibly dark. Our heroes had never left their small hometown; the world suddenly seemed so much larger to them than it ever had before. Larger and much, much more terrifying. As the hooded riders drew ever closer, I looked up and blinked. The Florida sun shone brightly through the window, cast long shadows along the floor. I blinked. It wasn't raining; it wasn't even night! How?

My brain had fallen so deeply into the world of hobbits and rings that it took a few seconds for the world of sunshine and family vacations to kick in. It was such a small moment, but I remember how far away from the window I was sitting when it happened, what the chair felt like beneath me, the particular quality of afternoon light that happens when the sun sinks low enough to look eye to eye with those tall buildings by the sea. Somewhere inside, I knew that the moment had changed me, that a new kind of magic had revealed itself, and the world would never be the same again.

Reading Is an Invitation

Making graphic novels is a kind of magic.

While I'm drawing, I can visit the world of the story.

I can meet the characters, spend time with them like they're real.

I get to live inside the story as I'm telling it.

But it always ends.

Finishing a graphic novel puts that world into a snow globe.

It's frozen, protected behind glass.

Until...

Other people read the book, and I can see in their faces:

They have also gone to the world.
They have also met the characters.

And I realize the story isn't mine anymore; it belongs to them.

It belongs to you.

by Molly Knox Ostertag

72. Reading can lead you to your dream job

by Micol Ostow

It was 1999. I was twenty-three, and working as an editorial assistant for a small, serious publisher of very serious, important nonfiction books. After college, I'd applied for jobs in women's magazines and publishing. And when an offer came from a huge publishing house, I jumped.

It didn't take long for me to realize that as much as I loved books, I definitely wasn't serious enough for the division of the company where I was working. Slowly, I started to wonder if I belonged in book publishing at all.

Didn't editors have to be very, very serious about their books, all the time, in order to publish serious, important books that would change people's lives?

That was my fear. But it was misguided. And improbably, it was *Buffy the Vampire Slayer* who came to my rescue.

A friend who worked in the production department knew I was a huge fan of the show. When one of our mysterious, cloistered paperback divisions released a companion guide to the show, she left a copy on my desk as a gift. I couldn't believe such an intensely comprehensive book about *a television show* existed in the world. More to the point—it was a *fun* book, in spite of being richly detailed and rigorous.

I had to know who at this company was creating books like this one. Fortunately, the name of the editor who'd worked on the book was listed on the inner copyright page. I memorized it, fantasizing about one day meeting this beautiful genius.

Six months later, I was looking for jobs in magazines—I'd given up on being a "serious" nonfiction editor. I was sure, by that point, that I was in the wrong line of work.

And then.

I was waiting for an elevator when I saw a sign listing new jobs in the company. Specifically, I noticed an opening in one of our paperback divisions—Pocket Books. I decided to apply for the job.

Little did I know, I'd applied to assist the very same editor of that *Buffy* book I'd fallen in love with.

Thrilled as I was to finally be meeting that editor, it was only when I walked into her office that I realized I'd stumbled into the holy land—a place where *fun* books were taken very, very seriously. Her shelves were filled with names of authors I remembered from my sleepaway camp days. Christopher Pike. Francine Pascal. Bruce Coville. It was an entire category of books I'd completely forgotten since aging out of sleepaway camp. And remembering it was no less than magical.

It was the dream job I'd never known I'd wanted. It was kismet. And as it turned out, I *am* extremely serious about books—but particularly the fun ones. I edited them for a long time before I began writing my own. And I realized that in fact, books are where I've always belonged.

73. Reading is a special superpower

by Rodman Philbrick

I was eleven years old when my own special superpower was revealed to me. My younger brother and I were avidly reading Eleanor Cameron's Mushroom Planet books, about two boys who build a spaceship and voyage to a nearby planet. Like the boys in the book, we decided to build a spaceship of our own, out of old boiler parts and pieces of junk. Luckily my mother interrupted us before we got to the gunpowder rocket-fuel stage. But the books unleashed in me not only a craving for more books, but an understanding that stories can be powerful things that extend into the real world. Instinctively I understood that books could change my life. That same year I came across *The Phantom Tollbooth* by Norton Juster, and the deal was done. I knew who and what I wanted to be. An author! In sixth grade, I secretly began to write stories and send them out to magazines—secretly, because I thought announcing I was a writer would set me apart, as indeed it would have in the very small town where I grew up.

My dream of getting published and joining the ranks of the writers I so admired did not come easily, as it almost never does. Possibly because I began with absolutely no clue about how to write a publishable story. We all know the only way to get to Carnegie Hall is to practice, practice, practice, and the only way to acquire the skills of a professional writer is to write, write, write. And read, read, read. And then write some more, learning how to focus your imagination, coaxing your characters to life.

For me the reading was what drove the writing. One could not exist without the other. There were no creative writing courses available to me. Books were where I learned how to listen, observe, and study. They were my own private university. My instructors were Mark Twain, Joseph Conrad, Ray Bradbury, and Ursula Le Guin. Guest lecturers included Flannery O'Connor, Fyodor Dostoevsky, Flann O'Brien, and Louisa

May Alcott. Raymond Chandler was a regular at the student pub, as was Joseph Heller. (They used to arm wrestle, but neither of them ever won.) The winner was me, sitting in a corner, observing and absorbing. Learning by reading, by letting a chorus of author voices show me how it was done.

In middle school I wrote hundreds of short stories and poems. All were rejected. I wrote what I thought was a novel in high school. Not good enough to find a publisher. I did have a poem published in an actual magazine in my senior year of high school, and found that I was too embarrassed to show it to anybody. After struggling through nine unpublished novels, I finally figured out how to write in a way that engaged the reader, and was eventually able to earn a living doing the thing I love most in the world.

So thank you, authors; thank you, books. I couldn't have done it without your help and inspiration. Thank you, thank you, thank you!

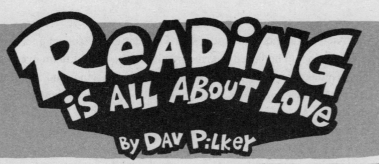

Reading is All About Love
BY DAV PILKEY

I never needed anybody to tell me I had reading problems.

I figured that out on my own.

MAYBE I SHOULD SEND YOU BACK TO KINDERGARTEN!!!

My teacher helped.

I never needed an assortment of labels to zap my confidence, either.

Dyslexic

Challenged Reader

Reluctant Reader

Slow Reader

I learned to hate books all by myself.

On the rare occasions when I **DID** find something I wanted to read...

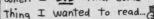

...it seemed as if my choices were never good enough for my teacher.

That's Not Your READING Level!!!

CAN'T YOU find something more SUBSTANTIAL?

You've ALREADY READ THAT BOOK A HUNDRED TIMES!

THAT'S NOT A REAL BOOK!

But just when everything seemed hopeless, my mom came up with a **GREAT** idea:

Instead of focusing on **WHAT** I was reading...

...She made sure **THAT** I was Reading.

PUBLIC LIBRARY

So she got me a library card...

...and let me choose **Whatever** I wanted to read— with **NO Judgment.**

It didn't matter if it was a magazine...

...or if it was below my reading Level...

...or if I'd already read it a **Hundred Times.**

My mom believed that if I read what I **Loved**...

...I might develop a **LOVE** for Reading.

And she was **RIGHT!**

LOVE was the Key.

Love Led to habits...

...and habits Led To Skills.

Skills that Continue to this day.

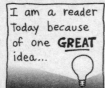
I am a reader Today because of one **GREAT** idea....

...and a lot of **LOVE.**

Dav Pilkey 2017

75. Reading is a bouquet on paper

by Andrea Davis Pinkney

Dear Langston Hughes,

Do you know what you've done?

You are the one
who saw this Black girl struggling
to see herself
on the pages of the books she read.

That's right,
her brown-skinned dreams,
they just weren't there
in the stories that weren't *her* story.

No, *un-uh*,
this girl's reflection didn't shine
in the book-mirrors
she was given.

It was 1976.
This child was lonely.
And hungry.
And the only one
in her classroom
who had brown-girl cheeks
and eyes wide open in a world
that didn't seem to notice
she needed to read books that said: *You. Are. Here.*

And so,
her reading hunger grew.

And so,
she wanted words that could feed
the deepest places
of a starving soul,
wanting stories that spoke her truth.

To make matters worse,
the rumbling way down in her belly
made her swallow hard,
and brought on a tummy ache
she came to call
"That Day When I Felt the Pain of Not Wanting to Read."

But then—*hello!*—*you* came.

Langston Hughes.

Bringing good news!

It was a spring afternoon when you knocked on my heart's
    front door.

And there it was. A special delivery. Just for me.

A book!
Your book!
And *my* book, too.

Yours *and* mine.

That book, filled with your poems, was *ours*.

Because, you see, Langston, *you* saw *me*.

Through *you*, Langston Hughes,
I felt the power of *we*.

Through *you*, Langston Hughes,
I learned to love to read.

The book, *that* book.
Its title was simple.
But its gifts were a plentiful mix of everything I needed.

Selected Poems of Langston Hughes

That book selected this kid who'd been in pain.
That book *chose* me,
and *changed* me
and *saved* my life as a reader.

That book.
given to me by a special teacher.

Like you, Langston, she knew what I needed.

That book,
with its curled pages
and warped cover,
stained and decorated with library dust,
was the mirror that nourished the growling,
empty places deep down in me.

Langston Hughes,
in the wide-open eyes of this sweet-cheeked child,
your poetry's power made reading come alive.

Your word-music filled me up,
made me love to read.

You invited us to hold fast to dreams.

You introduced beautiful Ruby Brown, golden like the
    sunshine.

You showed everyone the wonder of a crimson trickle in the
    Georgia dusk.

You, Langston Hughes,
painted a bouquet filled with the colors of Cuba, Haiti, Harlem,
    Jamaica, and the Bronx.

Like the brightest flower,
that book—*our* book—met me face-to-face,
nose-to-nose,
smelling so fine.

Your bouquet-on-paper
was as bright as the warmest day in May.

When you, Langston Hughes, came to call,
hunger's roar slipped away.

Bye-bye, brown girl in pain.
Hello, blooming middle school poet!

Time to grow away from the growling, empty ache.
Time to gobble up books!
Time to chow down on reading!

Dear Langston Hughes,
I still own that dusty, tattered, selected poetry collection.

(Never returned what has now become my BBF—my Best
    Book Friend.)

And speaking of bests,
here's the best part of your May Day book-bouquet
and the selections that you, Langston Hughes, always deliver:

Somewhere, right now,
your words are lighting up the eyes and filling the bellies
of budding poets
who are spreading their petals to others.

And together, we see ourselves.
And together, we love to read!

76. Reading puts a light in your eyes

by Sharon Robinson

My love of reading began as a child. A good book exposed me to a world beyond my own experience. Stories brought clarity of past struggles and achievements to life. I related to any story with adventurous female protagonists. My mother encouraged this love for books by creating a library in our home and reading books with us before bedtime. If we asked her a question or begged for a new dog, Mom sent us to the set of encyclopedias to do research before she'd seriously entertain our request.

But . . . most of the characters in the books of my childhood were white. Honestly, I didn't realize what was missing until my freshman year at Howard University. Our assigned readings expanded my thinking and spoke to my heritage. I devoured Kafka's *Metamorphosis*. It made me unafraid of my own transformation since arriving at this incredible black college. At nineteen, I was away from home for the first time and enjoying the freedom to move about the world in a new, unrecognizable form. That same year I read *The Autobiography of Malcolm X* and Maya Angelou's *I Know Why the Caged Bird Sings*. Books that spoke to me as a young black woman. Stories that drew me out of isolation and into the light.

Now, as a children's book author, I've seen that same light in children's eyes during a reading from and discussion of one of my stories. Like the girls who look up to me in surprise and wonder at my honesty in *Child of the Dream: A Memoir of 1963*. I imagine them thinking, *Did she just say that out loud?*

I love reading letters from young readers. One of them wrote: "I learned that you're an activist. I have a 'Dream Big.' I want to stop child abuse. It really HURTS me more than it hurts them." Fans of *The Hero Two Doors Down* write and tell me that they are like the main character, Steve Satlow. Boys and girls who put themselves in Steve's place and imagine becoming friends with their favorite sports star. And there are letters that talk about Jackie Robinson and ask deep and basic questions about the man they've learned to admire. Many are relieved that their idol was also a loving father.

Books can entertain, lift our spirits, inspire us to make a difference, and be the best person we can be. I recently received a letter from a fifth grader from New York. He wrote, "I am writing to you regarding permission to use some information from your book, *Promises to Keep*, in my book. When I am done with the book, I am going to send it into Scholastic in New York City to try and get it published."

I hope he does.

77. Reading leads to fantastic collaborations

by Madelyn Rosenberg and Wendy Wan-Long Shang

E-readers, those slim devices that serve as an all-you-can-read buffet, are a great invention. You can get a new book when you finish a book at ten o'clock at night—without getting out of bed. You can go on vacation without lugging a bag just for books (hey—we like to be prepared!).

But let's face it, e-readers have one major drawback:

It's hard to see what other people are reading. Even if you're wearing your glasses. Even if you tilt your head and twist your body and lean. You can't read the title, or even see the cover to give you the faintest idea of what the book is about.

A book is like a badge, a T-shirt that says I LOVE SLOTHS or RECYCLE. It tells you what a person is interested in. If you spot someone reading a worn-out copy of your favorite book, the chances of you becoming friends go up exponentially.

We met in a writers' critique group, which is an interesting way to get to know a person. Sharing your writing, opening yourself up to criticism, offering your thoughts on someone else's writing—it's a crash course in Getting to Know You on a Deep Level. We ended up getting the same literary agent, and sold our first books within a few months of each other.

We liked what we saw in each other's writing, so it was only a matter of time until we got the idea to write a book together. Writing with a partner is a risk, though. A leap of faith. So a little sign that we were meant to do this? We'd take it.

We were having one of our many rambling conversations, engaging in what Madelyn calls Playing Tennis Badly, when the subject of young adult novels came up. When we were growing up, the category of "young adult" books was not the healthy genre it is today. After a certain age, you slipped into the adult section—or, in our case, you stole books off your mother's nightstand.

As we came to find out, we had stolen the *same* book, *Class Reunion*, from our moms as one of our first forays into adult books. *Class Reunion* is about four women who go to college together, and about their very different lives afterward.

We had our confirmation that we should write together, and from that partnership came *This Is Just a Test*, a book about a Chinese-Jewish boy named David Da-Wei Horowitz who worries about his bar mitzvah, his battling friends, and, you know, world peace. While we were editing, we talked in half sentences. We could decipher each other's barely coherent texts and emails. When we turned the book in, our own agents said they could not tell who had written what, and with very few exceptions, neither could we.

Then, for our first presentation on *Test* together, we independently created collages of books we loved as kids. We had three of the same books, down to the covers. As a bonus, we'd each picked a Judy Blume book. It was another sign. Who were we to ignore the fates? We wrote another book together, *Not Your All-American Girl*, about David's younger sister, Lauren. It's about figuring out who you could be, over the noise of so many people trying to tell you, rightly or wrongly, who you should be. The cover is purple, like our own dog-eared copies of *Are You There, God? It's Me, Margaret*. If you see someone carrying it, we hope you'll strike up a conversation. You might find a partner in crime. Or a lifelong friend.

78. Reading is a rope in a deep well

by Pam Muñoz Ryan

I wasn't always a reader. I didn't grow up with many books in my home and I don't have memories of people reading to me. It wasn't until the summer before fifth grade that books and reading captured me.

My family had moved across town and I was new to the neighborhood. On one of my bike rides, I discovered the small East Bakersfield Branch library near my house. Initially, it was nothing more than a destination and not necessarily a place I went to *read*. It was someplace to which I could say I was going, and not be questioned by my parents. I was by myself, without my little sisters. It was quiet. Best of all, in the 107-degree heat of the San Joaquin Valley, it was air-conditioned.

It was inevitable that, sooner or later, the books would hold me hostage. Stories are powerful that way. I wanted to know what came next. I wanted to turn the page. I didn't want the story to end. As I walked between the stacks, I sometimes imagined that adventures were waiting to leap from the confines of the books so they could grab me and pull me in. Eventually, that's exactly what happened, with *The Swiss Family Robinson* by Johann David Wyss, *Treasure Island* by Robert Louis Stevenson, and dozens by Marguerite Henry, including *Misty of Chincoteague*.

Reading kidnapped me. I carried books to kitchen tables, to the car, and (secretly) to church. I was as strong, adventurous, and determined as the protagonists in the stories. Or as long-suffering. I tried on many lives other than my own and hung on to stories I loved, reading them over and over, as if they were a rope in a deep well.

Recently, I ran into the woman who had been my best friend during seventh and eighth grade. She reminded me that when we walked home from school together, I sometimes read out loud to her. I had forgotten! I suppose because *I* was lost in the book and everything else was incidental. But to her, it was still a vivid memory. She admitted that after I read chapters to her, she would often go to the library and check out the same book so she could read it in its entirety. Without knowing, I tempted her curiosity, and she was caught, too.

As I made my way through junior high, books carried me away, at least temporarily, from the wrath of mean girls, isolation, tallness, big feet, miserably hot weather, and a town that late-night talk show hosts called "the armpit of the world." It wasn't, at least to me. I coped through books, discovering them at a time of my life when I was insecure, struggled socially, and was searching for how and where I belonged in the world.

It is no surprise that I now often write for readers who are the same age that I was when books made the biggest difference in my life.

79. Reading gives breath to a new whisper

by Aida Salazar

We read to listen to the whispers of universes we have never
known.

We read to unfasten the clasp of memory trembling with
excitement to be set free.

We read to find joy laughing out loud in the rain beneath a
polka-dot umbrella.

We read to pull back the truth like blankets off a sleepyhead
baby brother.

We read to witness beauty bloom delicate as dew on a blade
of grass.

We read to bend with time like taffy in our mouth.

We read to excavate questions waiting like blue sea glass
buried in the sand.

We read to stuff our faces with suspense like popcorn at a movie.

We read the map others have traveled and see our own
crooked prints speckled on the paths.

We read to awaken the ghosts asleep in our basements.

We read to fill our minds from the well of inspiration, bucket
after bucket.

We read to hear the voices of our ancestors sing a lullaby in a
       language we don't remember.

We read to feel loss burst open our hearts with a sudden,
       painful theft.

We read to marvel at how love can mend what is broken in us.

We read to learn a secret folded into a paper airplane and
       flung through the air.

We read to see heroes emerge like triumphant birds from
       smoldering ash.

We read to meet goodness for a warm pancake breakfast.

We read to unravel the tangle of a problem and wind its
       solution into a perfect ball of yarn.

We read to know that ugly and pretty are twins who bicker
       for the front seat.

We read to make ourselves big with courage, look into the
       eyes of fear, and send it blasting into space.

We read to be lifted with power as justice does the right thing.

We read because we might just discover the story inside
       ourselves.

Then, perhaps, find the freedom to write it for others to read.

And give breath to a new whisper in the universe.

80. Reading can take you to different times and places

by Lisa Ann Sandell

I have always loved books that transported me to other times, other places. Growing up, I often felt like I didn't fit in, like I was an outsider. So I looked to books to help me escape my reality. And in those moments, reading enabled me to forget about the troubles I was having with friends or bullies or school; I could dive into a story that let me travel in my imagination and shed all the worries that plagued me.

Stories of magic and adventure, of comradeship and characters who were on a quest to do something brave or beautiful, were my favorites. These types of stories moved me. And they still do.

I read hungrily and I read broadly—from Lloyd Alexander's high fantasy quintet, the Chronicles of Prydain, and Edward Eager's stories of enchanting adventures happening to regular kids in his Tales of Magic books, to the dreamy magic of Natalie Babbitt's *Tuck Everlasting* and the startling brilliance of Madeleine L'Engle's Time Quintet, and far beyond. The first time (of many) I read *A Wrinkle in Time*, I can still remember being struck, as if by a bolt of literary lightning, when I came upon this passage:

> *"Just be glad you're a kitten and not a monster like me." She looked at herself in the wardrobe mirror and made a horrible face, baring a mouthful of teeth covered with braces. Automatically she pushed her glasses into position, ran her fingers through her mouse-brown hair, so that it stood wildly on end, and let out a sigh almost as noisy as the wind.*

I had never read a character who expressed the exact same self-critical feelings that I harbored. Seeing myself in Meg Murry was earth-shattering.

For the first time, I began to feel that maybe I wasn't alone, maybe I wasn't a freak. That maybe there wasn't something wrong with me. Perhaps most importantly, this book, and all the others I devoured, let me see that the world, that life, held so many possibilities. That things could always get better and magic might turn up around any corner.

But it was the stories of King Arthur and his Knights of the Round Table that completely beguiled me. I loved the notion of a king who longed to build a better, more just land. The fact that these legends held up the ideals of justice and equality, honor and friendship as most essential, most meaningful, resonated deeply with me. These themes spoke of a better world than the one I saw around me, where people could be cruel and things seemed frequently, terribly unfair. But as I grew older, I started to wonder where the female characters in these Arthurian stories were. The women were featured as villains at worst (such as Morgan le Fay or Guinevere, who in turning her affections to Lancelot, her husband's best friend, is ultimately responsible for Arthur's and Camelot's demise); and they were victims, weak and helpless, at best (such as Elaine of Astolat, also known as the Lady of Shalott).

My favorite bit of storytelling magic? In reading so much and loving books so fervently, I was eventually inspired to tell my own stories. I got to explore the legend of Arthur anew, and in my own way—through the eyes of a female protagonist—in my novel *Song of the Sparrow*.

For every reader, young and old, I have one wish: May you, too, find inspiration and, above all, *hope* in all the stories the world has to offer.

81. Reading is human

by Allen Say

Before I learned what "aphorism" meant, I read one I never forgot: *Humans who don't read are half humans.* The stinging words comforted me because I was reading books when I should have been earning my daily meals.

Whoever said it made me wish I had thanked my mother for teaching me to read when I was five. Actually, she was trying to find a way to stop me from drawing on walls or running away from home, and reading worked. Books and scrap paper made me happy; I didn't need playmates.

When I was twelve, I lived alone in a one-room apartment in Tokyo, made two friends, and read the first Japanese translation of *The Voyages of Doctor Dolittle.* The adventures of the chubby English doctor who could speak with birds and animals filled me with enchantment I didn't know in real life.

At sixteen I left my boyhood in Japan and reset my life in America.

Conversation in English was a three-step act: decide what to say; translate in the head; say the words like Humphrey Bogart. Hoots and taunts. I never got over the stage fright.

For reading, I started with picture books for children—*Babar the Elephant* and *The Story of Ferdinand* are two I remember. I was a five-year-old again.

As I moved on to books without pictures, I got helplessly lost in a borrowed dictionary—looking up one word led to looking up ten new words that led to . . . I never returned the dictionary. *Doctor Dolittle* was written in English; I had to learn it.

One day I caught myself thinking in English. That was progress, but it made me think backward. I wondered how I could say an odd English phrase like "raining cats and dogs" in Japanese. That complicated my reading: two languages overlapped on the page and made unexpected patterns as on a double-exposed photograph. A reader with only one language wouldn't see it. I thought about writing my own stories.

I looked up at the mountain of English words and got altitude fright. Then I heard a voice in my head: *Tell your stories with drawings and put captions on them.* Picture books! I would be a kind of ventriloquist with pictures as his dummy. When the dummy breathes and talks, the audience doesn't see the ventriloquist. I wrote some captions and got off the stage. Let the dummy do the talking.

And here I am back on the stage and asked what books meant in my life. Stage panic at eighty-two . . . then my old habit turns the big question around: If I hadn't read the books I had read, what difference would that have made to my life?

Books are the maps for the journeys of your mind and heart.

Without them, I would be an armchair explorer with no place to explore: I wouldn't have seen the great lighthouse of ancient Alexandria or the domes of Samarkand or walked to the end of the Silk Road.

Saddest of all, I wouldn't have met the many unforgettable people made of words I could have gotten to know by reading their minds and hearts.

Take away reading from my biography and you'll have a nameless old man in a flat world with short history and no enchantment. A half human.

82. Reading can turn a classroom into a magic carpet

by Augusta Scattergood

I grew up in a small southern town where we spent summers roller-skating and playing baseball in the park, swimming in our town pool, and playing hopscotch and tag till dark. In the winter we had no snow or ice-covered ponds. Until my fifth-grade teacher, Mrs. Wiggins, read *Hans Brinker, or The Silver Skates*, I didn't know anybody who owned a pair of ice skates, much less knew what to do with them. But while she read that book, all twenty-five of the kids in my class were holding up the dike and saving our families right along with the characters. I was ten, and the only time I'd traveled that far was inside the pages of a book.

Almost every day, often after recess with the window shades pulled down and our spelling lists tucked inside our desks, all the people and the pets inside the pages of *Tom Sawyer*, *Old Yeller*, or *Call It Courage* became our friends. My teachers read books aloud—all the time. The Mississippi River flowed not far from my town. We swam in its oxbow lakes, caught catfish from the muddy banks, even dreamed of river rafting. It was high school when a teacher opened *The Adventures of Huckleberry Finn* and took us up that river.

If I chose a book to read to myself, it was likely Nancy Drew or a biography about a famous person. But if Miss Cane or Mrs. Turner or Mr. Lipe or anyone read a book aloud, it didn't matter if it was mystery or history or anything in between. I couldn't wait to listen. Soldiers went to war, someone dear died in *Little Women*, dogs died in lots of stories. And when our teacher got to the sad parts, all of us, even the toughest boy who'd hit fly balls on the playground minutes ago, dropped our heads to our desks and wiped away secret tears.

After the teacher tucked the bookmark into the end of a chapter and raised the window shades, sun poured in. The blackboard, erasers, and chalk were still there and the globe hadn't moved from its corner. The classroom hadn't changed. We had. Listening, we'd been somewhere special. We'd painted a fence, loved a horse, skated to win.

Later, as a librarian, I read *Bridge to Terabithia* and cried right along with my fifth graders. Recently, I read *Merci Suárez Changes Gears* to a young friend and remembered the stories my own grandmother told. Now, as an author, I read for inspiration. *Flora & Ulysses* and *Love That Dog* and *Shiloh* and my favorite, about a pup-on-the-loose named Wishbone—they all remind me of why I love reading. It started with the excitement and delight in hearing stories read to me. It started when a teacher turned our classroom into a magic carpet, sweeping us to places we'd never been.

83. Reading can help you survive

by Eliot Schrefer

A few years ago I was visiting a teacher friend in Seattle, and she invited me to talk to her class about my books. On the drive to her school, she told me about how almost all her students were refugees from Cambodia, and that their families were struggling to make ends meet, so often the students would drop out of school in order to work to financially support their parents. I started to feel worried. Who was I to talk about the love of reading when these kids didn't have time to go to school, much less read books?

Still, I went ahead with my presentation, about my book *Endangered*, which is a survival story about a girl surviving wartime in Congo with an orphan ape by her side. I show research videos of my time in Africa during that presentation. The videos of apes being goofballs, which usually get audiences laughing, were met with no reactions.

Feeling sheepish, I asked if the kids had any questions. There was just a long silence.

Then, finally, one of the boys raised his hand and asked, "If a chimpanzee and a gorilla got in a fight, who would win?"

"Oh," I stammered. "I guess the gorilla, because they're stronger."

"Okay, okay, what if it was three chimps against two gorillas, but they had a little monkey sidekick, too?"

We did this for a while—primate cage-match questions.

A shy young woman in the front raised her hand, then asked, "If the bonobo apes have these female alliances that keep everyone safe, is there any way that humans could do the same thing, to prevent war?"

I was stunned by the question, especially coming from someone whose family had fled wartime to come to a new country. This wasn't an academic or poetic question—it was a matter of personal life strategies, of figuring out how to survive from a work of literature. The cage-match questions had been a version of the same thing.

As I took some pictures with the students and said goodbye, I realized that I'd been making some wrong assumptions. I'd thought that students will only read if their essential needs are met, and that we need to help students really struggling to find the space to start reading. But that's not really it. Those students fighting for survival also need books *during* that fight. As a writer, I don't get to decide what they take out of the book. They'll find what's useful for them in it. That's what humans do with stories.

84. Reading is a magic you can experience and create

by Victoria Schwab

I did not grow up loving books. I could read well enough, but by the age of eleven, I hadn't yet found a book that truly transported me, that gave me that feeling other people spoke of, of forgetting who you are, where you are, when you are. That feeling of words on paper blurring, replaced by the story in your mind. It sounded like magic, but it was a magic I didn't know.

And then, one day, my mother's friend called us. She said she was in a bookstore in Southern California, said there was a lady there signing a book for kids my age, and should she pick up a copy for me? My mother waffled, knowing I was drawn more to sports than stories, but in the end, she said yes. And what arrived in the mail the following week was a signed copy of *Harry Potter and the Sorcerer's Stone*. Needless to say, I found the magic I was searching for in those pages, and never looked back. I became a lifelong, avid reader, thanks to my mother's friend who happened to be at one of J.K. Rowling's early signings.

Falling in love with reading really was magic. And because I'm a Slytherin, I also marveled at the power of it all. If it was magic to read a story and forget yourself, it was power to *write* a story and make someone else forget. From that moment forward, I knew I wanted both—to read and to write, to experience that magic myself and create it for other people.

85. Reading shows you how words and pictures are different sides of the same thing

by Brian Selznick

Words and pictures have always been connected for me. When I was very young I had a lisp. Instead of saying "ssss," I said "thhh," so my parents sent me to a speech therapist. The therapist drew a snake in the shape of an S and I had to fill the snake with S's. Every time I drew an S, I had to make an "esss" sound with my tongue in the right place (behind my teeth)—not an "ethh" sound (with my tongue sticking out between my teeth). Forever after that I thought of the shape of the letter S, the sound of the "sss," and the snake itself as the same thing. For me there was no difference between the word, the picture, and the sound.

Sssssnake.

I remember reading many books by Remy Charlip around this time. He was my favorite author and illustrator. I loved how words and pictures worked together in his books. In *Fortunately*, we follow the adventures of a boy named Ned who is invited to a surprise party. Ned has to travel far and wide to get there and has many setbacks, including an airplane with an exploding motor, a cave crawling with tigers, and an ocean filled with sharks. Every time something good happens to Ned (*"Fortunately he could swim."*) the picture is in color. Every time something bad happens to Ned (*"Unfortunately there was a hole in the parachute."*) the picture is in black and white. Each turn of the page moves us from something good to something bad, from a picture in color to a picture in black and white, from "Fortunately" to "Unfortunately." The words, the pictures, and the mood all become one and the same. I thought that was really exciting, and I think it was Remy Charlip's work that taught me to really love books.

Years later, when I was making my book *The Invention of Hugo Cabret*, I met Remy Charlip in real life. I was so happy to tell him how much his books meant to me when I was a child. During the conversation I realized he looked very much like one of the main characters in my story, the filmmaker Georges Méliès, so I asked Remy if he would pose as the character. He said yes. That means that every time you see one of my drawings of Georges Méliès, you are really looking at a drawing of my favorite childhood writer and illustrator, Remy Charlip.

But more than Remy's face is in my book. The lessons I learned from him are also there. Remy showed me how words and pictures are different sides of the same thing, like the snake I'd drawn as a small child. Besides being a children's book writer and illustrator, Remy was also a teacher. He believed that everyone could make pictures and use language, even if they don't think they can write or draw. I agree with him. Think about it. If you read a book with *no pictures*, you will create pictures in your mind of everything you read, even if you never draw them on paper. (Right now I can write the word *elephant* and I bet you can see an elephant in your mind!) Also, if you look at pictures in a book and try to describe them to someone, you will think of words to use pretty easily. And the exact pictures you imagine, and the specific words you say, will be different from everyone else's on earth. In fact, telling stories that combine words and pictures is what humans have done throughout history, all the way back to the dawn of time. In the caves of Lascaux, the pictures on the walls tell the story of a big hunt. Tens of thousands of years later, we have emojis on our phones that can also tell stories! These little images can express moods, ideas, and entire conversations in a single picture half the size of your fingernail.

Caves and phones are fine places for stories, but I prefer books, and I think that's why my books are filled with images of, and stories about, other books. *The Invention of Hugo Cabret* was a celebration of the cinema, but ultimately it was about the power of books. When you finish reading that book, the object in your hand, the book itself, becomes part of the story, almost like a magic trick.

That kind of magic, the ability to take ideas and stories and make them real, to share them with the world, is the gift Scholastic has given all of us. After I graduated college, I worked as a bookseller at Eeyore's Books for Children, in New York City. The most important aspect of my job was getting the right story into the hands of each person who came into the store. That's the same job publishers have, on a global level—creating and sending out stories so they end up in the right hands. I've made a lot of books with Scholastic. Maybe some of them have ended up in your hands. One is about a boy who lives behind a clock in a train station, another is about a Deaf girl who runs away to New York, and a third features a boy who survives a shipwreck. I even had the chance to draw another snake when I was asked to illustrate the covers for the twentieth anniversary of Harry Potter!

Now *this* book has made its way to your hands. The words and pictures you hold, created by one hundred different authors and illustrators, make up a larger story, one that I'm proud to be a part of. And even though you'll close these covers eventually, the stories in your mind, the words you think of, and the pictures you imagine, will never stop.

86. Reading is good news

by David Shannon

Well, maybe it's old-fashioned, but I love to read newspapers. I love how they smell, and what they sound like when you turn their pages and snap them into a nice, flat page to read. Of course, you can roll one up and whack stuff, too, or you can fold it into a hat. But mostly I like that they're full of all kinds of stories. I love to read stories.

I started reading newspapers when I was a kid. The first thing I read was the sports section, especially the box scores of all the baseball games. You can tell a lot from a box score if you know how to read them. You can almost picture the whole game in your head. I always went right to the Giants game to see if Willie Mays had hit a homer—he was my favorite player—then I read all the other games.

Later on, after I became an illustrator, I read all about what was going on in the world because that was my job. Newspaper publishers would send me a story and I was supposed to paint a picture of what it was about, with maybe a little twist that would get people interested and help them understand the subject better. Usually I only had about twenty-four hours to come up with something, so it was important to already be pretty familiar with what was happening.

Now I write and illustrate books for kids, but I read newspapers more than ever! I still like going over all the baseball box scores and keeping track of who the good guys and the bad guys are in the world and what they're up to. But I don't just read the front page news or the sports section—I love reading the whole paper all the way through! I like to find out how much snow fell up at the ski mountain or if my softball game's going to get rained out. I like looking at the all the photographs, the funny cartoons and the cool pictures that other illustrators are doing now. I like reading about music, and artists' new paintings, and what books and movies are coming out. There are also brand-new discoveries—like a planet that might have life on it, or a cave with prehistoric remains.

And then there's all the other stories. People do a lot of crazy things, and they're all there in the newspaper. Or maybe it's something weird that's washed up out of the ocean, or a pig that fell in love with a turtle! Sometimes I get ideas for a book from these stories. Every day, I get to learn new stuff and I never know what it's going to be! That's why I love reading newspapers.

Reading is...

Matilda was the novel that opened my mind to the transcendence of reading.

I felt like I discovered a supernatural power of my own.

...And I knew that thousands or millions of other kids must feel it, too.

Reading is the gateway to a human collective conscious.

Reading is one of humankind's most lasting and sturdy legacies.

Books teach us. They make us cry and laugh and feel what it means to be human.

They show us who we've been, who we are, and who we will become.

That is why I write.

Reading is the impetus for our evolution as people and I want to be a part of humankind's ongoing legacy.

Picking up a book is no less than being a part of our biggest achievements as a species.

Reading is cosmic.

by Kevin Sherry

88. Reading can take you to a place called hope

by Peter Sís

When you are locked in a room, behind the walls of the city and the country.
When you have no place to turn for help—

Then reading can take you to the place called hope, to imagination, to humanity and to the future.

89. Reading gives you invability

by Jordan Sonnenblick

Books have always been like oxygen to me. I can't imagine life without them. When I was a kid, the stories in books, and especially in comic books, often seemed more real to me than the events that were going on around me in "real" life. This sometimes got me in trouble, like this one time in third grade when I was at my friend B.J.'s house.

B.J. has been my best friend since preschool. B.J. and I have always shared books. I discovered comics first, when we were in first grade and my dad's barber had *Avengers #138* (Stranger in a Strange Man) and *Daredevil #112* ("Murder!" Cries the Mandrill). B.J. got me into DC comics last year, when he discovered the Legion of Super-Heroes. I lend him my science fiction novels, and he brings me piles of fantasy books. We spend hours on top of his bunk bed arguing over who would win in different battles. Would Shazam beat Thor? What would happen if Gandalf from *Lord of the Rings* fought Darth Vader? Could Saturn Girl from the Legion of Super-Heroes read Professor Xavier's mind?

These arguments get pretty heated. I once got sent home by B.J.'s mom after B.J. and I started wrestling to decide whether Superboy was stronger than Ultra Boy. The issue was very complicated, because we had a list of each hero's powers, and we saw that Ultra Boy had invulnerability. We didn't know what that was. We couldn't even pronounce it. So when B.J. said Superboy was probably stronger than Ultra Boy, there was only one way to figure it out. I jumped on him and shouted, "Invability! I win!" He yelled, "Heat vision! You lose!" I got him in a headlock and shouted, "Invability beats heat vision!" He rolled over so he was on top of me and grunted, "Super breath!"

Which has to be Superboy's dumbest power, by the way.

This went back and forth for a while, but eventually B.J. pushed me against the wall with his feet. I grabbed B.J.'s gold necklace, pulled on it, and screamed, "Invability!" B.J. pushed off from me so he was hanging halfway off the bed. Then his necklace broke and he fell.

He wasn't even hurt, but his mom was super mad! She said his necklace, which had the Hebrew symbol *chai* on it for good luck, was a family heirloom, whatever that means. The next thing I knew, I was sitting in my mom's car on the way home, getting yelled at by her, too.

Apparently, super mad beats invability.

B.J. once told me he is going to be a doctor like his dad, and that one day he is going to invent a cure for cancer. I know what I want to do with my life, too. I'm going to write a book someday. I hope kids just like me will read it and feel like they have invability, too.

90. Reading is full of small magic

by Maggie Stiefvater

Cats with wings. Paintings that became doors to other worlds. Whispers in the deadest of night from the deadest of people. Growing up, the books I pulled off the shelf always had magic in them.

I recall the books of my childhood more strongly than the houses we lived in. My father was a navy doctor, so when I was a kid, we moved, and we moved again, and we moved some more. Coast to coast and back again, and then, even after he got out of the navy, from town to town, hospital to hospital. We didn't really have a home; we had houses. Mostly I remember the libraries—my mother always signed us up for new library cards, first thing—and I remember the books.

I'd sit in the library stacks for hours, picking out every volume I could find with a unicorn or UFO sticker on the spine, the universal librarian method of marking fantasy and science fiction books. Magic, magic, I always wanted to read about magic.

The best sort of magic, in my opinion, was small magic. Sure, I liked dramatic fantasy worlds and huge monsters and dueling wizards as much as anyone, but the stories that stuck with me were ones with a more intimate scope: books about chemistry sets that turned out to be full of peculiar magic spells, like in *The Ogre Downstairs*, or cats who were ordinary, apart from being able to fly, like in *Catwings*, or girls who lived lives a lot like mine, but haunted (*Wait Till Helen Comes*).

Books with big magic were great; they were escape. Literary vacations. That was good enough in a pinch. But books with *small magic*, believable magic, magic that might really happen—well, they changed the way I looked at the world. They made me look for small magic even after I closed the pages. They made me look for small magic in the real world.

Because of these books, I'd listen for fairy music in the woods behind our subdivision, conjure thunderstorms with backyard spells, search the ocean's coast for water horses, play Scrabble with the ghosts in our attic, time travel for just a minute or two in the basement of a historic house. I did this small magic and more, because once I got in the habit of looking at the world that way, I couldn't really stop. The truth is, there are all kinds of tiny, eerie miracles humming through life once you've been taught to look. And that was true for me no matter what zip code I lived in, no matter which house we were moving to or from.

Where did I grow up? I grew up here: learning that the wind whistling through the chimney doesn't have to be just the wind, suspecting that the creature you saw in the woods behind your school could have been something more than a deer, and realizing the small, strange girl that was you might just be a hero waiting to happen.

This is what books did for me: They made small magic my home.

91. Reading is an adventure!

by Geronimo Stilton and Elisabetta Dami

Dear rodent friends!

Actually, no . . .

Dear rodent reader friends!

Hello, everyone!

Please, let me introduce myself . . . My name is Stilton. Geronimo Stilton. I'm your faithful mousey friend and editor of the *Rodent's Gazette*, Mouse Island's most *famouse* newspaper.

Yes! It really is me! In fur and whiskers!

Chunky cheesy bites, but if today isn't the day I wanted to tell you about how much I love reading. *Squeak!*

And would you like to know who else loves to read? My "mom"! She helps me write my books about Mouse Island and New Mouse City. If you don't know her, I'll introduce you: My "mom" is Elisabetta Dami, and she's been writing children's books for years.

She always lends a paw (*Oops!* A hand!) to create our adventures. And every single one is sweeter than cheesecake and more breathtaking than blue cheese! They're also popular all over the world! Did you know they've been translated into forty-nine languages?

Lots of our thrilling stories are inspired by the trips my "mom" and I take together. You see, we're very curious about the different cultures and traditions of the world. The whole world!

And there are lots of laughs in our books, too. That's because Elisabetta and I often have a good laugh together, and every time we write a book, we want to share the positive way we see the world.

Our stories are about values as well—things like integrity, loyalty, sincerity, honesty, kindness, courage, friendship, respect, love of nature . . . I'm sure you've heard of all of them! They're a kind of magic compass: When things get a bit hairy, they help us decide the right path to cheese! I *am* sorry! *Choose!*

Anyway, one of the most important values for Elisabetta and me is our love of reading. We think books are *mousetastic*! That's because books are faithful friends.

Books keep us company always and everywhere, and make us feel all sorts of different things: They can make us laugh out loud, they can touch our hearts, they can make us dream . . . and all without ever giving us time to get bored!

Just like good friends, books give us so much without ever asking for anything in return. They offer us everything, but only when we're ready and willing to gobble up all those good things. Every book has an important message for us, and it's up to us to listen!

Books are friends that take us on the biggest adventure there is: the adventure of reading. Because—word by word, page by page, chapter by chapter—every book takes us for a ride on the wings of imagination. I give you my cheesy word on it!

Books, like good friends, also help us get to know the world a bit better. And by showing us our own feelings and hopes, they help us get to know ourselves better, too.

So, let's meet again soon in a book! We'll set off together on a new *mousetastic,* fur-raising adventure!

Hooray for books! Hooray for reading! Hooray for rodents!

Big, warm, melted cheesy goodbye hugs to everyone! *Squeak!*

92. Reading leads you to some real heroes

by R.L. Stine

People ask me what books I read as a kid, and I'm always embarrassed to answer, "I didn't read books. I read only comic books."

My friends and I carried around stacks of comics with us, and we would swap them and pore over them together, study the art and the storylines, and spend hours deciding which to add to our collection next. I had eclectic tastes back then—*Dick Tracy*, *Looney Tunes*, *Little Lulu*, *The Lone Ranger* . . .

Then one day, my mother dropped me off at the little library on Main Street. (I grew up in Bexley, a suburb of Columbus, Ohio.) A librarian was waiting for me at the door.

She said, "I know you like comic books, Bobby. I have something else I think you will like."

She led me to a shelf of Ray Bradbury stories—and changed my life forever.

I dug into the stories. I couldn't believe how imaginative they were, how wonderfully written, how surprising, and most all of them with tricky twist endings.

Ray Bradbury turned me into a reader. I read as many of his stories as I could find. Then I moved on to Isaac Asimov, Robert Sheckley, Frederik Pohl, and Philip K. Dick.

From science fiction, I began to read fantasy novels. And then the Greek myths, fairy tales, the Norse legends.

I never forgot that librarian and the amazing favor she had done for me.

Many years later, when I was an author and the Goosebumps series had become popular all over the world, I had a chance to meet Ray Bradbury. I spotted him eating a hot dog in a publisher's booth at the L.A. Times Book Festival.

I knew I had to say hello to him. He was so important in my life. But I was horribly nervous. I walked up to the booth, and I was shaking like a kid. I stuck my hand out to shake hands with him, and my voice was high and trembly as I blurted out: "Mr. Bradbury—you're my *hero*!"

He turned around, shook hands, and said: "Well, *you're* a hero to a lot of other people!"

What a wonderful thing to say. It was one of the most amazing moments of my life.

And it never would have happened if that librarian in that tiny library hadn't decided to show me some books she thought I might like.

93. Reading brings you unexpected friendships

by Francisco X. Stork

Over the years, I have been asked by certain books to be their friend. I don't know how a book knows that I need a friend at that particular time. Their offers of friendship arrive in unexpected ways. I'll be walking aimlessly in a bookstore or library when, suddenly, I am drawn mysteriously to the one who will become my friend. Later, when I start reading, I understand why a book befriended me just then.

My first friendship with a book happened when I was thirteen. Charlie Stork, my adoptive father, had recently died in an automobile accident. I had known Charlie only a brief time. Seven years before, he was traveling through Mexico when he fell in love with my single mother, Ruth Arguelles. Soon after Charlie and Ruth married, we came to El Paso, Texas, where there were better economic opportunities for our little family.

A few months after his death, my mother had to return to Mexico to care for my grandfather while I stayed with a neighbor. The days were sad, but the nights were worse. I missed horribly the father and good friend that Charlie had become.

I don't remember how the book came into my hands. It was a thick, old-looking book with a frayed cover. The language was old Spanish and there were many words I did not understand. I read every night until my eyes closed, and if I awoke in the middle of the night, the book was there, within my reach.

There was something about the adventures of the crazy old man who thought himself a knight that brought me warmth and light. The dialogues between the old man and his funny squire made me smile for the first time in a long time. I felt less alone when I was with them. And when I closed the book, their courage and liveliness to pursue their quest stayed with me.

I am old now, but Don Quixote and Sancho Panza are still friends. I visit them every couple of years and they remind me again of the light they brought to me when I was thirteen. Over the years, I have also become friends with Miguel de Cervantes, their creator. Like all good friends, we admire our differences and delight in the things we have in common. I understand the kind of person he is, and when I read his book, I feel as if he wrote it for that thirteen-year-old boy who needed a friend.

94. Reading lets you have whatever power you want

by Tui T. Sutherland

If you had to choose between flying or invisibility, which one would you pick?

What if you had to choose between telepathy, teleportation, or time travel?

Or what if you could shape-shift into a dragon . . . or a fox?

What if you didn't have to choose—because you could have all of the above?

That's what I think reading is: the closest we ever get to having superpowers. When you're reading, you can be a flying telepathic dragon, a shape-shifting teenager, or a magical fox. You can teleport to Antarctica (with *The White Darkness* by Geraldine McCaughrean) or the fantasy kingdom of Attolia (in the books by Megan Whalen Turner); you can time travel to 1970s New York (*When You Reach Me* by Rebecca Stead), ancient China (*Where the Mountain Meets the Moon* by Grace Lin), or a spaceship in the future (*Sanity & Tallulah* by Molly Brooks and hundreds more!).

We all wonder what other people are thinking, don't we? I'm endlessly curious about what's going on in other people's heads. Why are they doing what they're doing? Do they think like me? Do they worry like me? Do they want the same things? I feel like, with books, we can actually find out. We're inside the author's brain with her, finding out how she thinks her characters think. Is there anything closer to telepathy than that?

If I had to pick one of the powers above, I must admit I'd probably choose teleportation. I'd never be late again! Plus I could zip to amazing faraway places whenever I wanted. There are so many places I haven't been yet—but I feel like in some ways I have, because of authors like

Mitali Perkins, Tracey Baptiste, Linda Sue Park, Juana Medina, and Amy Tan, whose stories take us all around the world.

And isn't it just like being invisible when you read a scene that you would never see out in the world? A scene between a family at home, or teachers in their secret teacher lounge, or a girl writing her first story alone in her room?

I think reading doesn't just give you the experience of having superpowers; it actually grants you the most important superpower of all: empathy. Once you've been the lonely boy whose adopted family treats him cruelly (the Harry Potter series by J.K. Rowling), or the kid who knows she's something different on the inside than what people see on the outside (*George* by Alex Gino), or the girl who's embarrassed about the clothes she has to wear because her parents can't afford anything else (*Front Desk* by Kelly Yang)—you'll always have their voices somewhere inside you. You'll always be able to imagine yourself in their place. You're building the power to understand what another person is feeling—to look across the room at a person who seems totally different from you and think, *They have a story, too. It's different from mine, but it's just as real as mine.*

And hopefully, the more stories you read about kids (or dragons) changing the world, the more you'll think, *I can do that, too!* Because you can! Even if your actual superpowers are kindness instead of invisibility, empathy instead of flying, and hope instead of teleportation.

So keep reading, take those superpowers, and go save the world! ☺

95. Reading is whatever you want it to be
by Shaun Tan

WHY DO YOU READ?
let's ask some
random strangers...

I never know what I'll find!

I'm researching Ancient Roman
blood sports!

I like books about ponies.
You gotta problem with that?

I'm a bookworm.
What more do you need to know?

I like urban paranormal Victorian
steampunk speculative romance.
A lot more than your dumb questions.

I can live many lives.

I like the words.
I like the pictures.

I can take my time.

rarf!

I'm growing my own wisdom.

It turns a boring commute into an ADVENTURE.

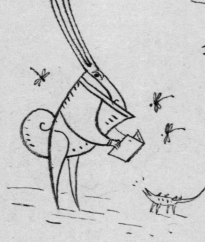

I enjoy seeing things from a different point of view.

...mnrf.. can't talk... gnrr...

* I love language.

I love all your
crazy Earthling antics!

I like short stories.   I like BIG stories.

Nobody can tell me what to think.

96. Reading is rewarding . . . even when it's hard to do

by Lauren Tarshis

My dad was a writer when I was growing up, and every morning I woke up to the song of his typewriter . . . *clickclackclickclackDINGclickclack-clickclackDING!* We didn't have much money, and my dad seemed to work way more than my friends' dads, who put on ties and got on the train to work in banks and offices in New York City.

But I knew that my dad loved what he did. And when he would travel, which was often, I would go into his tiny, messy office and stand in front of his beat-up typewriter and think, *I want to be a writer when I grow up.* But then the next thought would be, *But that's impossible.* And it *was* impossible. Totally impossible, I was sure.

Because I had a secret back then, and the secret was that I couldn't read a book. I could read words just fine—sound them out, read them aloud, no problem. But put all those words on pages with characters and plots and by around page three all those words would be buzzing around in my mind like crazy flies, making no sense at all. I didn't know I had a reading challenge. I just thought I wasn't smart. And just like my too-big feet and my too-frizzy hair, I was sure nothing could be done to stop those word-flies from buzzing around my brain.

I was too ashamed to tell my parents or my teachers or my friends. So I kept it from them. Somehow I stumbled along, faking my way through school, never doing very well.

Meanwhile, my house was filled with books, and my parents loved to read. My friends were all big readers, especially my best friend, Michele, who was always talking about her favorite book characters. Fern from *Charlotte's Web*. Kit from *The Witch of Blackbird Pond*. Charlie from *Charlie and the Chocolate Factory*. The way Michele talked about these characters, they seemed like flesh and blood. It was like

Michele was always getting invited to parties and hanging out with all these fascinating people. They made her laugh and think and care and feel inspired. I wanted to meet them! And I was locked out, cut off.

This went on until I was fourteen, this secret struggle, and that's a whole other long story. But finally, my first year of high school, I figured out how to read a book. The first book I read was *A Tale of Two Cities* by Charles Dickens. Somehow I discovered that if I read every paragraph two or three times, and took notes, I could keep the information straight in my head. Reading that book was the first time I had the experience of *reading*: of entering a new world, traveling through time, connecting to characters who came to life in my mind and my heart. It was even better than I'd imagined.

Over the years, I've read all the books Michele and my other friends used to talk about—and many, many more. I've met thousands of characters from different times, places, and worlds. And now I'm writing my own books, bringing to life characters I can only hope you will talk about with your friends as though they're real.

And as I'm writing this now, I can hear the sound of my dad's beat-up typewriter in my mind, that *clickclackclickclackDINGclickclackclickclackDING!* echoing from all those years back.

I am remembering how I stood in front of my dad's typewriter, dreaming of being a writer. Knowing it was impossible. Never imagining I could be wrong.

97. Reading is something you can pass down

by Sarah Weeks

Reading was always one of my favorite subjects in school, but it never occurred to me that I might grow up to become an author. When I was young, I wanted to be a ballerina like the girl in a book I loved called *Ballet Shoes*. Or maybe a clever detective like Nancy Drew, following clues and solving mysteries no one else could figure out. The future was full of promise and the books I read offered an endless supply of possibilities. Every Saturday my dad would take my sister and me to the Dairy Queen to get vanilla cones dipped in chocolate, and after we'd finished our ice cream, we'd head over to the Ann Arbor Public Library to pick out our books for the week. Everybody in the Weeks family was a reader. It wasn't unusual to find us all sitting around the living room with our noses buried in a good book. My father was an English professor and a wonderful storyteller, but it was my mother who read to me every night before I went to sleep. I remember loving picture books like *Curious George* and *Harry the Dirty Dog* and, as I got older, chapter books like *Charlotte's Web* and the Little House series.

Years later, when I had children of my own, I looked forward to reading to my two sons at bedtime the same way my mother had read to me. Well, not *exactly* the same way. Sometimes I would change the words to make them laugh or make up a story of my own to amuse them. When they outgrew those silly made-up stories and learned to read on their own, that's when it dawned on me that maybe I ought to try writing my stories down so that other people's children could enjoy them at bedtime.

That was almost thirty years ago and I'm still making up stories today. One thing has changed, though—there's a new book lover in the family. My son Gabe began reading to his daughter Lulu even before she was born. I remember he called me one day to say that the baby already had a favorite book—one of mine! "How can you tell she likes it?" I asked, and he explained that whenever he read it to her, she would kick. I hope when she's old enough to read some of the books her gigi wrote, she'll feel the same way about *Glamourpuss* and *Pie* and *Save Me a Seat* and *Soof*. Lulu's parents read to her every night before they put her down to sleep the same way I read to my children and my mother read to me. Someday when Lulu has children of her own, I have a feeling she'll read to them too. Life is good and reading makes it even better.

98. Reading is a radiant web of words

by Scott Westerfeld

The same story that made me a reader also made me a writer. The two roles, after all, are part of the same web.

Charlotte's, to be specific.

The story of Wilbur and his spider protector is about friendship, of course. It's also about how children process their growing realizations of injustice, of loss and impermanence, and of death. But for me, *Charlotte's Web* was always about the power of the word.

Wilbur becomes a famous pig not through his great deeds or dazzling talents, but thanks to words. The adjectives that Charlotte weaves above his pen—*terrific* and *radiant*—are the sort that roll luxuriously off a kid's tongue when first learned. There's a relish to uttering our early "big" words. My niece, now seven, refers to everything even mildly interesting as *magnificent.*

As a child, I was also a relentless repeater of new words. My sisters rolled their eyes at how my latest pet adjective wormed its way into every sentence I spoke. It was probably solid teaching, repeating new acquisitions, but I had no conscious desire to increase my vocabulary. My repetition sprang from a sense that words are spells. They have power on the tongue; they are music in the air.

One of the tempting promises of reading was that more new words would be coming my way, ready to be deployed in daily life. And that they would bring me power.

Charlotte weaves compliments into her webs, but she isn't simply out to flatter Wilbur. She's out to rescue him from a death as inevitable as the seasons. That we can save someone with the right words at the right time—"I love you," "You are valuable," "Don't touch that wire!"—is the height of word magic.

Whenever we lose someone in the worst way possible, the question lingers in the air: "What could I have said?"

As I got older, the truth of Charlotte's story grew more complicated. Especially when I learned that words not only told stories, but possessed their own—the word *text* descends from the Latin *texere*, "to weave," and the great weaver in Greek myth was Arachne, who was transformed into the mother of all spiders for daring to out-weave the gods. Her name went down the same path, becoming the root of the word *spider* in Romance languages, and the scientific name of the order that includes them. The oldest stories are always right here, woven into our words.

We spin tales, we argue in threads, and good stories are yarns—all of it goes back to weaving. There's a godlike power in capturing a reader in a web of words, a divine pleasure in being captured.

But I was still surprised when I read *Charlotte's Web* to my niece last year, and encountered its last lines: "It is not often that someone comes along who is a true friend and a good writer. Charlotte was both."

Like a magic trick, the card I thought I'd chosen for myself was right there all along.

99. Reading gives you answers to questions you don't even know to ask

by Deborah Wiles

When I was a kid, my favorite room in our house was my father's study, with its bookcases across one wall that were filled with . . . knowledge. I was a nerdy kid who wanted to understand the world (I already loved it), and I learned early on that answers to the questions I didn't even know to ask were found in books.

So I pulled them off the shelf, one by one, and then, sprawled across the checkered rug in my father's study, year after year, I was educated.

My favorite series to scour was called *The Book of Knowledge: The Children's Encyclopedia*. I opened it at random and read about how the atomic bomb was made (which I am sure I remembered many years later when I wrote *Countdown*), or how cotton was ginned and manufactured (which I remembered as I wrote *Revolution*), or how to hike the Alcan Highway in Alaska (which I have not written about . . . yet).

My favorite book in my father's study was the *Reader's Digest Treasury for Young Readers*. I read that book cover to cover, many times. I read about how to make musical instruments "from odds and ends," how to identify birds, how television works, and—my favorite—"John Glenn's Day in Space." Which again led to *Countdown*, decades later. I think the mind stores away what it learns, against the day it might need that memory or that knowledge; at least I think that's what happened with some of what I learned in all those years of education. Who knew I would write about atomic bombs or cotton picking or the American space race? All I knew was that there was an immense pleasure to be had in reading and learning, and I was like a sponge, wanting to know everything there was to know about the world and who lived in it.

And I knew that I liked best books that had lots of ways to tell the stories within them, books full of pieces and parts, odds and ends of connective tissue that made up the whole. A puzzle here, a map there, some poetry, some directions.

So it felt natural to me, when I became a writer, to write stories that contained lots of connective tissue . . . like the letters, recipes, gossip columns, and obituaries that help tell Ruby's story in *Love, Ruby Lavender*, Comfort's story in *Each Little Bird That Sings*, and Emma Lane Cake's story in *A Long Line of Cakes*.

Like the scrapbooks full of photographs, song lyrics, newspaper clippings, quotes, and other primary source material I included in the Sixties Trilogy: *Countdown*, *Revolution*, and *Anthem*.

It would take many years of reading both fiction and nonfiction, and falling in love with characters in novels that I clung to like breath, before I began to understand how to write my own stories by combining my personal history with the history of the world. I'm convinced I write using this structure of bits and pieces and odds and ends that all fit together—because it was how I loved to read as a child.

I discovered those books I loved, and a direction for the writing years ahead, because—I now see—my father loved the world in the same way I did; because he wanted, just as I did, to understand the world; and because he gathered so many books close to him, so he could read to his heart's content, and learn. Just as I did, after him.

Thank you, Dad.

100. Reading is incarnational

Three poems by Jane Yolen

How to Get into a Book

Some people stride in at a galloping clip,
Some at a comfortable lope.
Some test the waters with hesitant toe,
Some slide down a book's slanting slope.

Some hop right in with a mile of a smile,
Some crawl so reluctant and slow.
Some fling themselves right into towering waves
And get caught in the strong undertow.

But me, I fall down the deep hole of a book,
Where I spend a long, comfortable time.
I don't care if the book is a memoir or novel
Or made up of rhythm and rhyme.

It's the bookness I crave, all the new worlds I find,
When I travel afar in the hold of my mind.

This Is Not a Book

This is not a book but a world,
trees like fists, thrust upward, bold.
Rivers snaking through the tall grass,
startled, winding, glassy, cold.

This is not a book but a city
a skyscraper of seems,
pothole of fears, cracked pavement
of promises, fueled by dreams.

This is not a book but a life,
throbbing with story,
an arc of decisions, a thwarting
of interests, climax of glory.

This is not a book, but my art,
my desires, my craft, my decisions, my heart.
This is not a book.

Incarnation

"Writing is incarnational"
    —Flannery O'Connor

Reading is incarnational, too.
I began this day as a Jane,
made my way through Dorothy,
finished as a flying monkey,
shook the alternate dust
of Oz from my shoes.
Tomorrow I plan to go sailing
with Billy Budd; hope that ends
rather better than the last time
we took to sea.

This incarnational thing
is hard on relationships,
finishing as they do
with the slap of a cover.
I get to go back to my own life,
and they get to stay inside theirs
till some godlight shines again
on their opening pages.
Which one of us will last?

That's the question.

Reading helps you grow!
by Raina Telgemeier

About the Scholastic Authors

Collectively, the authors below have written well over a thousand books, many of them for Scholastic. Among the titles listed, there are award winners, bestsellers, and many books that have become classics since they were first published. Because we only have enough space for a line or two for each author, the following is an incomplete list highlighting up to three of each author's Scholastic titles. Readers are encouraged to check out scholastic.com and the authors' individual websites to learn more about each author.

K.A. Applegate is the author of such generation-defining series as Animorphs, EverWorld, and Remnants.

Avi's many acclaimed novels include *The True Confessions of Charlotte Doyle*, *Nothing but the Truth*, and *Midnight Magic*.

David Baldacci is the author of the Vega Jane series that began with *The Finisher* and concluded with *The Stars Below*.

Blue Balliett's first novel was *Chasing Vermeer*, beginning a series that continued with books including *The Wright 3*. Her most recent book was the ghost story *Out of the Wild Night*.

Jim Benton started at Scholastic with the It's Happy Bunny and Dear Dumb Diary series. His current Graphix series is Catwad.

Judy Blundell is the author of *What I Saw and How I Lied* and, as Jude Watson, novels including *Loot* and many books in the 39 Clues series.

Coe Booth is the author of books for younger readers including *Kinda Like Brothers*, and YA novels including *Tyrell* and *Kendra*.

Ann E. Burg debuted with *All the Broken Pieces*. Her other novels include *Serafina's Promise* and *Flooded*.

Kacen Callender is the author of *Hurricane Child* and *King of the Dragonflies*.

Sharon Cameron's YA novels include *The Dark Unwinding*, *Rook*, and *The Light in Hidden Places*.

Angela Cervantes is the author of novels including *Gaby, Lost and Found*; *Me, Frida, and the Secret of the Peacock Ring*; and *Lety Out Loud*.

Lucy Christopher made her mark with her first YA novel, *Stolen*, and has since written novels including *Flyaway* (for younger readers) and *Storm-Wake*.

Joanna Cole and Bruce Degen are the team behind the Magic School Bus series, which launched in 1986 and published a new book, *The Magic School Bus Explores Human Evolution*, thirty-four years later in 2020.

Suzanne Collins is the author of the picture book *Year of the Jungle*, the middle-grade series The Underland Chronicles, and the YA series The Hunger Games.

Bruce Coville has been engaging young readers' imaginations for many decades with books including his Unicorn Chronicles series, and his *Book of Nightmares* and *Book of Monsters*.

Christopher Paul Curtis's novels for Scholastic include *Elijah of Buxton*, *The Madman of Piney Woods*, and *The Journey of Little Charlie*.

Edwidge Danticat's writing for children ranges from the picture book *Eight Days* to the Royal Diaries title *Anacaona, Golden Flower* to the YA novel *Untwine*.

Sayantani DasGupta launched her Kiranmala and the Kingdom Beyond series with *The Serpent's Secret* and continued with *Game of Stars* and *The Chaos Curse*.

Lulu Delacre's storytelling includes the picture books *Arroz Con Leche* and *Vejigante Masquerader* and the collection *Salsa Stories*.

Chris D'Lacey's fantastical series for young readers include The Last Dragon Chronicles and The Erth Dragons.

Jennifer Donnelly has spun many tales for young adults, including *Stepsister* and *Poisoned*.

Jenny Downham is the author of the YA novels *Unbecoming* and *Furious Thing*.

Julie Falatko is the author of the series Two Dogs in a Trench Coat, including such titles as *Two Dogs in a Trench Coat Go to School* and *Two Dogs in a Trench Coat Start a Club by Accident*.

Sharon G. Flake's many acclaimed novels include *Pinned* and *Unstoppable Octobia May*.

Aimee Friedman is the author of many YA novels, including *Sea Change*, *French Kiss*, and *Two Summers*.

Cornelia Funke has taken readers to many worlds in her novels, including *The Thief Lord*, *Inkheart*, and *Dragon Rider*.

Eric Gansworth is a poet and scholar, as well as the author of the YA novels *If I Ever Get Out of Here* and *Give Me Some Truth*.

Lamar Giles is the author of the mysteries *Overturned* and *Spin*, among other novels.

Alex Gino started their career with the novel *George*, and continued with *You Don't Know Everything, Jilly P!* and *Rick*.

Christina Diaz Gonzalez's writing for young readers includes the novels *Moving Target* and *Return Fire* and a forthcoming graphic novel.

Alan Gratz's works of historical fiction include *Prisoner B-3087*, *Refugee*, and *Allies*.

Melissa Grey is the author of many YA novels, including *Rated*.

Virginia Hamilton was one of the twentieth century's most highly regarded writers for children. Her writing for Scholastic includes *Her Stories: African American Folktales, Fairy Tales, and True Tales* and *The People Could Fly: American Black Folktales*, as well as many novels and picture books.

Karen Hesse is the author of such beloved novels as *Out of the Dust*, *Witness*, and *The Music of Dolphins*.

Tanuja Desai Hidier is the author of the groundbreaking novel *Born Confused* and its sequel, *Bombay Blues*.

Jennifer L. Holm and Matthew Holm are the brother-sister team behind the Sunny series, which Jennifer writes and Matt illustrates. The titles include *Sunny Side Up*, *Sunny Rolls the Dice*, and *Swing It, Sunny*.

Deborah Hopkinson's works of nonfiction include *D-Day: The World War II Invasion That Changed History*; *Titanic: Voices from the Disaster*; and *Shutting Out the Sky: Life in the Tenements of New York, 1880–1924*.

Alaya Dawn Johnson is the author of the YA novels *The Summer Prince* and *Love Is the Drug*.

Varian Johnson's books for young readers include *The Parker Inheritance* and *The Great Greene Heist*.

Jess Keating has written for readers of all ages, including the series Elements of Genius and Bunbun & Bonbon, and the picture book *Eat Your Rocks, Croc!*

Christine Kendall's debut novel was *Riding Chance* and her latest is *The True Definition of Neva Beane*.

Kody Keplinger's books include the middle-grade novel *Lila and Hadley* and the YA novels *That's Not What Happened* and *Run*.

Barbara Kerley is the author of such nonfiction picture books as *The Dinosaurs of Waterhouse Hawkins* and *Eleanor Makes Her Mark* as well as the novel *Greetings from Planet Earth*.

Sabina Khan is the author of *The Love and Lies of Rukhsana Ali* and the forthcoming *Zara Hossain Is Here*.

Kazu Kibuishi's Amulet series was one of the first in the Graphix imprint and has continued most recently with its eighth installment, *Supernova*. He also wrote the picture book *Copper*.

Amy Sarig King is the author of *Me and Marvin Gardens* and *The Year We Fell from Space*. She also writes YA novels as A. S. King.

Bill Konigsberg's YA novels include *Openly Straight*, *The Music of What Happens*, and *The Bridge*.

Gordon Korman published his first novel, *This Can't Be Happening at Macdonald Hall!*, with Scholastic when he was fourteen years old. Over four decades later, he is still publishing at Scholastic, with novels including *Restart* and *War Stories*.

Jarrett J. Krosoczka's work ranges from picture books to books in the Jedi Academy series to the YA graphic memoir *Hey, Kiddo*.

Kirby Larson is the author of the Dogs of World War II series, including *Duke* and *Code Word Courage*, and the Audacity Jones series.

Kathryn Lasky's series include Guardians of Ga'Hoole, Wolves of the Beyond, and Bears of the Ice.

Peter Lerangis wrote a number of books in the 39 Clues series and the novel *Smiler's Bones*, among many other works for young readers.

David Levithan has edited four anthologies of the best young writers and artists in America, drawn from winners of the Scholastic Art & Writing Awards, as well as co-edited the YA anthology *21 Proms*. He has worked at Scholastic since he was nineteen.

Sarah Darer Littman is the author of many realistic novels for teens, including *Want to Go Private?*, *Backlash*, and *Deepfake*.

Natalie Lloyd's enchanting novels for young readers include *A Snicker of Magic*, *The Key to Extraordinary*, and *Over the Moon*.

Tracy Mack is the co-author of the Sherlock Holmes and the Baker Street Irregulars series, as well as author of the novels *Drawing Lessons* and *Birdland*.

Carolyn Mackler has written the middle-grade novels *Not If I Can Help It* and *Best Friend Next Door*, as well as numerous YA novels.

Ann M. Martin's The Baby-sitters Club launched in 1986 and currently has over 180 million copies in print. Her acclaimed novels include *A Corner of the Universe* and *A Dog's Life*.

Wendy Mass is the author of the Willow Falls series, which started with *11 Birthdays*, and the Twice Upon a Time series, as well as other novels for young readers.

Patricia C. McKissack was, along with her husband, Fred McKissack, one of the most honored writers of fiction and nonfiction for young readers, for books such as *Black Hands, White Sails*; *Christmas in the Big House, Christmas in the Quarters*; and *Days of Jubilee*.

Kate Messner's writing for young people includes the Ranger in Time series and the novels *Capture the Flag* and *Manhunt*.

Ellen Miles is the author of the Puppy Place series, among other series for kids.

Sarah Mlynowski made her mark with the Whatever After series, and is also one of the three writers of the Upside-Down Magic series.

Jaclyn Moriarty has drawn a passionate following of readers for middle-grade fantasies like *The Extremely Inconvenient Adventures of Bronte Mettlestone* and YA novels including *The Year of Secret Assignments*.

Robert Munsch is one of Canada's most beloved storytellers, for books including *Love You Forever* and *Andrew's Loose Tooth*.

Jon J Muth is the visionary creator of such picture books as *The Three Questions* and *Zen Shorts* and the graphic novel *The Seventh Voyage*.

Walter Dean Myers was one of the towering figures in children's and young adult literature. He wrote over a hundred books in his career, including *Fallen Angels*, *Slam!*, and *The Glory Field*.

Jennifer A. Nielsen is the author of *The False Prince*, *A Night Divided*, and *Words on Fire*, among many other novels.

Garth Nix is one of the foremost writers of fantasy for young readers and young adults. His series include The Keys to the Kingdom and The Seventh Tower, and his novels include *Frogkisser!*

Michael Northrop's works for young readers include the novels *Trapped* and *On Thin Ice*, and the series TombQuest.

Daniel José Older is the author of the Dactyl Hill Squad series, the Shadowshaper series, and novels including the forthcoming *Flood City*.

Molly Knox Ostertag is the author and illustrator of the acclaimed Graphix series The Witch Boy, which includes *The Witch Boy*, *The Hidden Witch*, and *The Midwinter Witch*.

Micol Ostow has written books in the Riverdale and Mean Girls universes, as well as YA novels including *Popular Vote*.

Rodman Philbrick's first novel for Scholastic, *Freak the Mighty*, was published in 1998. Since then he has written many acclaimed novels, including *The Mostly True Adventures of Homer P. Figg* and *Wildfire*.

Dav Pilkey has reached tens of millions of kids through his series, including Captain Underpants and Dog Man, as well as picture books including *The Paperboy* and *Dog Breath*.

Andrea Davis Pinkney is the author of such monumental works as *Marvin Rising: Requiem for a King* and *With the Might of Angels*.

Sharon Robinson's many works for Scholastic include the nonfiction book *Promises to Keep: How Jackie Robinson Changed America*, the novel *The Hero Two Doors Down*, and the memoir *Child of the Dream*.

Madelyn Rosenberg is the author, with Wendy Wan-Long Shang, of *This Is Just a Test* and *Not Your All-American Girl*.

J.K. Rowling first published with Scholastic in 1998 with *Harry Potter and the Sorcerer's Stone*.

Pam Muñoz Ryan's novel *Esperanza Rising* is celebrating its twentieth anniversary in 2020. She is also the author of such acclaimed novels as *Echo* and *Mañanaland*.

Aida Salazar launched her career as a novelist for young people with *The Moon Within*. Her second novel, *The Land of the Cranes*, is being published in 2020.

Lisa Ann Sandell's fiction for young adults includes *Song of the Sparrow* and *A Map of the Known World*.

Allen Say's remarkable career as a writer and illustrator includes the memoirs *Drawing from Memory* and *Silent Days, Silent Dreams* and numerous picture books, most recently *Almond*.

Augusta Scattergood is author of *Glory Be*, *The Way to Stay in Destiny*, and *Making Friends with Billy Wong*.

Eliot Schrefer is the author of The Ape Quartet, which began with *Endangered* and *Threatened*, as well as books in the Spirit Animals series.

Victoria Schwab writes novels for all ages. Her middle-grade novels include *City of Ghosts*, *Tunnel of Bones*, and *Everyday Angel*.

Brian Selznick wrote and illustrated such genre-defining books as *The Invention of Hugo Cabret* and *Wonderstruck*, and illustrated such picture books as *When Marian Sang*.

Wendy Wan-Long Shang is the author, with Madelyn Rosenberg, of *This Is Just a Test* and *Not Your All-American Girl*. Her solo novels include *The Great Wall of Lucy Wu*.

David Shannon keeps getting kids to say yes to his books, including *No, David!*; *A Bad Case of Stripes*; and *Duck on a Bike*.

Kevin Sherry is the author and illustrator of such series as The Yeti Files, Remy Sneakers, and Squidding Around.

Peter Sís's illustrated work includes the picture book *Robinson* and the art for Pam Muñoz Ryan's novel *The Dreamer*.

Jordan Sonnenblick made a generation laugh and cry with his debut, *Drums, Girls & Dangerous Pie*. He has since written many novels, including *Falling Over Sideways* and *The Secret Sheriff of Sixth Grade*. His memoir of his own fifth-grade year will be published in 2021.

Maggie Stiefvater's spellbinding YA novels include those in the Shiver and Raven Boys series, as well as *The Scorpio Races* and *All the Crooked Saints*.

Geronimo Stilton and Elisabetta Dami were first published by Scholastic in 2004 with *Lost Treasure of the Emerald Eye*. Over a hundred books in numerous series have followed.

R.L. Stine's hallmark horror series Goosebumps launched in 1992 with *Welcome to Dead House*. It is still going strong, most recently with the Goosebumps Slappyworld series, almost thirty years later.

Francisco X. Stork is the author of many praised works of YA fiction, including *Marcelo in the Real World*, *Disappeared*, and *Illegal*.

Tui T. Sutherland rode a dragon onto the scene with *The Dragonet Prophecy*, the first book in her epic Wings of Fire series. A Graphix version of Wings of Fire has also been wildly popular.

Shaun Tan's unique works defy categorization, as they compel readers young and old. His illustrated books include *The Arrival*, *Tales from Outer Suburbia*, and *Cicada*.

Lauren Tarshis has brought history to life for millions of young readers with her I Survived series.

Raina Telgemeier is the trailblazing author and illustrator of graphic memoirs such as *Smile* and *Guts*, and graphic novels including *Drama*.

Sarah Weeks is the author of a number of acclaimed middle-grade novels including *Pie*, *Honey*, and *Soof*.

Scott Westerfeld is one of the biggest names in speculative fiction for children and young adults. His series include Impostors and Horizon.

Deborah Wiles invented the genre of the documentary novel with her Sixties Trilogy. She is also known for the Aurora County novels, including *A Long Line of Cakes*, and her first work for young adults, *Kent State*.

Jane Yolen has shown one of the widest ranges, and has had one of the widest reaches, of anyone who's written for children in the past hundred years. She has written everything from picture books (including the How Do Dinosaurs series) to fantasy novels to young adult books, in both poetry and prose.